# A Turn In My Belly

## Discovering Yourself

A Road To Spiritual Recovery

_____

Angel Domingue

A Turn In My Belly

Copyright 2013 by Angel Domingue

# *Presented*

**To**

_____

**From**

_____

**Date**

_____

_____

_____

# Special Thanks

I thank you God for giving your only begotten son, Jesus Christ, who died for me so I can have a new and eternal life, and a beautiful relationship with you, God. I thank you God for giving me the precious gift of *The Holy Spirit* who has helped me throughout my life and given me the courage to write this book. I thank you God for giving me a testimony to share. I want the world to know how great you truly are, God. Words cannot express how grateful I am to know that you chose me. I am grateful for your unconditional love. I pray that people who read this book will come to know you in a more intimate way and will make the decision to become born again.

# Dedication

I dedicate this book to all who have a desire to change their life for the better and to grow spiritually. This book is also dedicated to my mother Briceida Ryan, my brothers Andrew Dominguez and Kirk Ryan, and to my sister, Audrena Dominguez; to my nieces Sophia Barraza and Taylor Vernali, to my nephews Andrew, Anthony Alexander, and my great nephew Andrew Dominguez, and to each member of my family. I thank my Church home, Bayside Of South Sacramento, Lee-Anna Postnikoff and the Postnikoff family for supporting this project. I thank Kathryn Mattingly, Tara Bodeker, and Kevin Anderson for helping me with the editing of this book. I thank my sisters in our small group. I thank the Women of Aglow International. I pray that each and every one of you have success in your journey fulfilling your purpose here on earth. Special thanks to my pastor Bishop Sherwood C. Carthen you will be missed but never forgotten. I love you all very much.

**Angel Domingue**

# Table of Contents

# Foreword

If you have received this Bible Study, then you indeed are blessed by the hand of God. He is reaching out to you through this step-by-step journey into a new life. Perhaps you will find it in your hands during your darkest hour, in the exact moment you are crying out for help. God is that help. Angel Domingue is an 'Angel of God' in how she has put together this instructive manual for bringing (or bringing back) to Christ those whom He has every desire and need to receive. His lost children.... And those who have been led astray.

May you, as the recipient of this booklet, realize the impact it can have on your life if you will only allow it to. Read, write, pray and study according to its instruction and be transformed. Become the person you have always wanted to be – loved and loving, whole and wholesome, productive and happy.
All the wisdom and guidance, all the heartfelt sharing and truths within this study can literally transform you from a lost soul to a soulful person singing praises to God because He has healed your mind and body, your spirit and your life.

More importantly, the love with which Angel has constructed these pages does not even begin to cover the love you can soon have for your Father in Heaven, who loves you in return, always and unconditionally, forever until the end of time... if you will just accept Him into your heart and use this study to develop a relationship with Him, your Lord and Savior.

Kathryn Mattingly
Author of Benjamin
@Amazon.com

**To get more Information about this book  "A Turn In My Belly" write:**

Angels On Board Prison Ministry

P.O. Box 247121

Sacramento, Ca 95824

angelonline@att.net

# Preface

A Turn In My Belly is inspired by my own experiences and those of other people—people who have suffered with addiction, domestic violence, trauma, abandonment, and the myriad of unexpected things that life brings. People who were able to recover despite their losses, misery, and pain. Each person who inspired this work was able to rebuild a new life, continue living out their purpose, and find true happiness. We all want to recover in a lost world. To do that, we must learn to successfully work through the wreckage, even when we feel it is hopeless. A Turn In My Belly tells the story of a true spiritual experience that can be achieved by any of us when we focus on the unseen.

# Introduction

A Turn In My Belly is a guide and workbook to help you answer some of life's most difficult and important questions, and to learn how to find the answers that are already inside of you. We are but wounded soldiers—fully equipped and highly intelligent. No one is more capable than you. This workbook is designed to help you put your life in perspective, and to help organize your Journey.

You will seek Me and find Me when you search for Me with all your heart

**(*NASB*, Jeremiah 29:13)**

# 1. Getting Honest

We all have regrets that make us look back and realize the mistakes that caused pain and hurt to ourselves and to the ones we love. We continue to judge ourselves and still feel shameful, we feel that we do not deserve a happy, prosperous life, because when looking back it reminds us of our failures. We all have a life story that has some regrets. So when we learn about God and His promise, we may feel that it does not pertain to us because of what we have done or experienced. Why would God help me after what I did? Wouldn't He rather help someone who made better choices? Someone who is not addicted to drugs? A good mother or a great father? Someone who is not in and out of jail? Someone who is happy with life? Wouldn't God rather work with that perfect married couple? The answer is NO. We may not think of all the great people God helped and used, but each one of them admitted to having regrets, shame, guilt, anger, and pain.

None of the Biblical characters helped by God were perfect. God made David a King even though he was a murderer and had an affair (2nd Samuel 11:1-16) Moses was a murderer as well. Moses killed an Egyptian who was beating a Hebrew slave. The Bible states that he did so "after looking around to make sure no one was watching," which indicates this was a premeditated act. This was before God used Moses to get his people to the Promise Land. Noah abused alcohol, drinking until he passed out and was found naked by his sons (Genesis 9:20-22) Joseph was a victim of child abuse by his brothers (Genesis 37:24-36) God protected Rahab, who was a prostitute (Joshua 2:1) Samson had long hair and was a womanizer (Judges 13) The Samaritan woman was divorced more than once (John 4:3-42) Martha worried about everything (Luke 10:40) The Disciples fell asleep while praying (Matt. 26:40-41) Peter denied Christ (Luke 22:54-62) Job went bankrupt (Job) Naomi was a widow (Ruth 1:3) Jonah ran from God (Jonah, Isaiah 37) Elijah was suicidal (1 King 19) Gideon was afraid (Judges 8) Jacob was a liar (Genesis 27) Abraham was old (Genesis 17) Paul, then known as Saul, was a "zealous" Pharisee who "intensely persecuted" the followers of Jesus. (Galatians 1:13-14)

Each one of the people God used for his glory made bad choices just like us. It is time to get honest and really look at your life—the good and the bad—and ask yourself if you have really given God a chance. Did I truly seek my creator like I sought relationships with people? Did I seek God like I did when I was seeking drugs or the best-looking clothes? Did I seek God like I was seeking a good career or job? Did I seek God like I was seeking approval from people? Did I truly seek God from my heart? Many times the answer is no.

God has asked us to seek Him, and only then we will find Him. Why would we not want to find our Creator? Many times the distractions of life get in the way of us building a relationship with God. So much is thrown at us from all sides, and society has brainwashed us into thinking that we should look and be a certain way for acceptance, But God looks only at the heart.

Some of us say that as soon as we get our lives together, get a job, leave this man or woman, or stop using drugs, we will start seeking God. Meanwhile, time is quickly going by and we are becoming older, unhappy and worst off. Let's be honest and look at the people we have spent time with; we see death and sickness and sometimes destruction. It is time to get honest about the way your life is going. Is it working? Has anything changed? We sometimes feel angry and lose control of our emotions. Some of us bring on our own anxieties because we are not feeding our spirit, we are feeding the outer, trying to grab onto what we think we need. And then we want a quick fix to feel good—sexual addictions, shopping addictions, gambling, or drugs, etc....

Doctors are here to help us and should be respected. People who are truly ill need prescribed medication. God created some people to become Doctors to take care of us and provide us with the care we need, and God will even use Doctors to take part in keeping us alive longer. However, some of us are not honest with our healthcare professionals. For example, we go to great lengths to receive a prescribed drug that we really do not need. We do this because we want to feel like anything but ourselves. We are too afraid to face the fact that we have messed up or that our lives are out of control.

Do you keep saying, "This is it; I am going to change my life," only to fall into the same old bad habits? Cycles like this leave us angry, but also emotionally and physically tired. They leave us not believing in ourselves, and if we cannot trust ourselves, how can we trust anyone else? To truly change, the first thing you need to do is get honest with yourself. Be truthful about whatever you did wrong, own it and make the change. God grieved when He seen the wickedness of humankind. However He made a change despite the pain and you can too. Look at the verse from Genesis:

> The Lord saw that the wickedness of humankind was great in the earth, and that every inclination of the thoughts of their hearts was only evil continually. And the Lord was sorry that he had made humankind on the earth, and it grieved him to his heart. So the LORD said, "I will destroy man whom I have created from the face of the earth, both man and beast, creeping thing and birds of the air, for I am sorry that I have made them". But Noah found grace in the sight of the Lord. **(NKJV, Genesis 6:5-8)**

Even God had to start over when He did not care for the way things turned out. He did not quit, but instead found something good in what He had created by finding favor in Noah.

Make a change right now by deciding to seek God for the first time in your life. Get honest with yourself and surrender. Share what has gone wrong in your life. Because when we get honest and admit our faults and mistakes, we can be free. You cannot start over if you cannot admit a change needs to be made. It's time to feed your spirit and inner self and to start the healing process. We have to build a relationship with God because it is impossible to get out of our wreckage without our creator.

But when you pray, go into your room, close the door and pray to your Father, who is unseen. Then your Father, who sees what is done in secret, will reward you.

**(*NIV*, Matthew 6:6)**

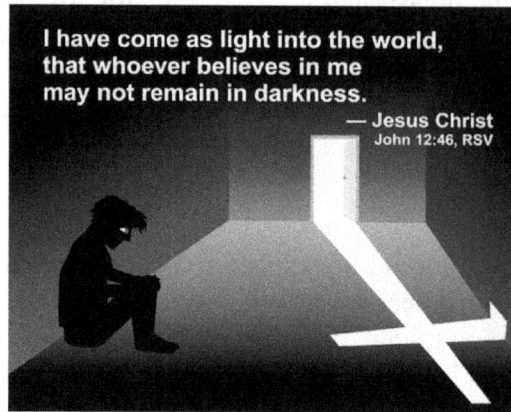

Perhaps you are not sure that you really believe in God. Just think—you believed in that bad relationship you were in, and that turned out to be a lie. You believed in taking drugs to help you feel better about yourself and life, and that made things worse. You believed in people who let you down or betrayed you. You believed in your job, then found yourself laid off. A lot of us who once followed God have since stopped coming to God. So perhaps we went a route that we knew was not what God asked of us. We were disobedient, and now we find ourselves facing the consequences of our life choices. We are all guilty, and we need God. God will not force us to come; He gives us free will. We must invite God into our lives and ask Him to be the pilot, not the passenger.

There is no specific prayer that we must say when we wish to speak to God. Just imagine God is standing in front of you. Be honest and sincere about how you feel, and invite God into your life. Use your own words. You can write it down first, if you prefer, and then say it.

### Example Prayer

*God, I am coming in faith. I am so alone and afraid. Change is not easy for me. God, I need to change my life. Please come into my life. I know there is someone greater than me, and that's you, God. I want to know you and your precious son Jesus Christ. I believe you raised Him from the dead for my sins. Please bring Godly people into my life and give me the knowledge and wisdom I need to survive in this world. Please take away these sinful cravings and this pain. Give me your peace. I ask these things In Jesus' name, Amen.*

If you declare with your mouth "Jesus is Lord" and believe in your heart that God raised him from the dead, you will be saved. **(Romans 10:9) (NLT)**

People who conceal their sins will not prosper, but if they confess and turn from them, they will receive mercy. (*NLT*, **Proverbs 28:13**)

**Getting Honest**

**Assignment:** Let's discuss some of the choices you have made that have caused problems in your life.

**Action:** Now that you know God will help you in any situation, regardless of your current condition, what would you ask Him to help you with? Write down at least three things that you would like to change now.

1)_____

2)_____

3)_____

4)_____

5)_____

Journaling your thoughts and feelings helps you process events and release emotions. Journaling is a great tool for problem solving. Throughout this workbook you will find pages to journal your thoughts and dreams, and to document prayer requests and testimonials.

# JOURNAL

*Write down your thoughts and share them with the group.*

Date: _____

_____

_____

_____

_____

_____

_____

_____

_____

_____

_____

_____

_____

_____

_____

_____

_____

_____

_____

_____

For God speaks again and again, though people do not recognize it. He speaks in dreams, in visions of the night, when deep sleep falls on people as they lie in their beds. He whispers in their ears and terrifies them with warnings. He makes them turn from doing wrong; he keeps them from pride. He protects them from the grave, from crossing over the river of death. **(Job 33:14-18) (NLT)**

# DREAM JOURNAL

Day: _____          Date: _____

Bedtime: _____          Time Awake: _____

**Dream Details:**

_____

_____

_____

_____

_____

_____

_____

_____

**Significance or Symbolism:**

_____

_____

_____

_____

_____

_____

# 2. Letting It All Go

Letting go is one of the hardest things to do, because nine times out of ten it will bring repercussions. It is hard for us to let go because we were designed to hold on and to be as one. When we were created, God never intended for us to be a lone ranger. When God created Adam, He wanted him to have a helpmate. God said in Genesis 2:18, "It is not good for the man to be alone" (KJV). So God made a helper for Adam. God wanted everyone to have someone. God is concerned for people who are lonely; loneliness was not God's plan for us. There are billions of people in the world today, and you can believe millions are lonely. What's even more significant is that God does not want to be alone either. That's why He created us. We were created to be in fellowship with God and man, but some of us left God out.

Some even use God as a scapegoat. God always waits for us to return to Him, because he knows it would be impossible for us to make it without Him. When God went back to the garden and could not find Adam, he called out to him. How must God have felt when Adam hid from God? God created Adam and loved him so much that he gave him paradise and made sure he was not alone. It is important to know God wants to give you paradise and love. God is not your enemy. But not putting God first was our tragedy. And not making God part of the family results in a dysfunctional family.

## The Dysfunctional Family

From Wikipedia, the free encyclopedia

A **dysfunctional family** is a family in which conflict, misbehavior, and sometimes child neglect or abuse on the part of individual parents occur continually and regularly, leading other members to accommodate such actions. Children sometimes grow up in such families with the understanding that such an arrangement is normal. Dysfunctional families are primarily a result of co-dependent adults, and may also be affected by addictions, such as substance abuse (alcohol, drugs, etc.), or sometimes an untreated mental illness. Dysfunctional parents may emulate or over-correct from their own dysfunctional parents. In some cases, a "childlike" parent will allow the dominant parent to abuse their children.

God is the creator of all. He wrote our operating manual for life. God knows what we need, and the first thing we need is a relationship with him. Some of us have gone through life not understanding that God has promises and protection in store for us, and some of us let it all go due to the ignorance of the unknown. We look around to see what society says. We look up to people with big money and big things—people who appear to be on the right path because of their material gain. We value people with money rather than people with God.

16

Do you remember the saying "Keeping up with the Joneses"? It was the desire to increase one's position and pocketbook. This desire only causes chaos. People now live above their means and find themselves not only spiritually bankrupt, but financially empty as well. Our Father in heaven is rich. God loves beautiful things, and what He created is good and beautiful. But we fell in love with the "wants," regardless of what it costs us. We look for love and happiness in cars, houses, money, clothes, relationships, electronics, drugs, jobs—anything and everything but God.

So can you be happy with the love of Jesus Christ? Is that enough for you? If you did not have all these material things, could you be happy in the complete forgiveness and unconditional love God has in store? Would that satisfy your heart? There is a time for wants, God said: "Delight yourself also in the LORD, And He shall give you the desires of your heart," (*NKJV*, Psalm 37:4-6). God also said, "But seek ye first the kingdom of God, and his righteousness; and all these things shall be added unto you," (KJV, Matthew 6:33) In these two verses, God is saying that He has your back. But do you have His? No one can give you what God has. When these material things go away, the love and happiness go to. Then you have nothing. The love of God will never leave you. His true love sustains us.

A person who gets caught up in serving another God will place anything above God. The love of money and the desire to get it at any cost is a gateway to living a lifestyle that is the opposite of our dreams. We have millions of people in jail due to the pursuit of money. Fathers and mothers become afraid of not having enough money to provide for their family. Some will get involved in drug trafficking. A therapist who could not make enough money in her practice started to prostitute at night to make more money. People in all walks of life do not put God first and find themselves compromising their morals and boundaries.

[36] For what shall it profit a man, if he shall gain the whole world, and lose his own soul?
**(Mark 8:36) (KJV)**

No servant can serve two masters; for either he will hate the one and love the other, or else he will be devoted to one and despise the other. You cannot serve God and wealth."

**(*NASB*, Luke 16:13)**

Matthew 13:44

### Letting It All Go

**Assignment:** Let's talk about the things that we are placing above God. Think about the choices you have made in life that have caused you problems. Are these some of the same things you put above God? Were they distractions that could be in the way of your fellowship with God?

**Action:** Make a list of the things you are placing above God. Use your journal to write down what you need to remove from your life, and other changes that need to be made.

1)_____

2)_____

3)_____

4)_____

5)_____

Journaling your thoughts and feelings helps you process events and release emotions. Journaling is a great tool for problem solving. Throughout this workbook you will find pages to journal your thoughts and dreams, and to document prayer requests and testimonials.

# JOURNAL

*Write down your thoughts and share them with the group.*

Date: _____

_____

_____

_____

_____

_____

_____

_____

_____

_____

_____

_____

_____

_____

_____

_____

_____

_____

_____

_____

_____

_____

_____

> For God speaks again and again, though people do not recognize it. He speaks in dreams, in visions of the night, when deep sleep falls on people as they lie in their beds. He whispers in their ears and terrifies them with warnings. He makes them turn from doing wrong; he keeps them from pride. He protects them from the grave, from crossing over the river of death. **(Job 33:14-18) (NLT)**

# DREAM JOURNAL

**Day:** _____          **Date:** _____

**Bedtime:** _____          **Time Awake:** _____

**Dream Details:**

_____

_____

_____

_____

_____

_____

_____

_____

**Significance or Symbolism:**

_____

_____

_____

_____

_____

# 3. Moving Forward

Moving forward is not always easy, but what is worse is not moving at all. Processing your life situations and where they have gotten you can be overwhelming. So much has happened in our lives that it can be difficult to know where to begin. Sometimes we may feel left alone to fend for ourselves—like we're in another country, looking at a sea of smiling faces, yet we have nothing to smile about. People ask you how are you doing, and you lie and say you are fine. When we feel this way, we often shut out those people that really care because we are scared to trust and be hurt again.

When you have finally made the decision to seek God's help, you must be willing to wait. We have spent many years making a mess out of our lives, so we cannot possibly expect a quick fix. I remember that when I started to move forward and make changes in my life, I drank too much, ate too much, loved too much, and lied way too much. I had no real friends as a result. I had too many secrets.

I was embarrassed to tell anyone I was running from my abusive husband who was an addict, and I played a part in the ongoing abuse by my choice of staying. I finally left after a near-death experience. At the same time in my life, I lost my younger brother, who suffered from a mental illness. When he drowned, I was so caught up in drinking and my own life that I could not be there for my baby brother. I carried a lot of guilt. I did not know how to communicate my feelings and emotions, so I stayed angry with everyone. I ended up homeless, going from couches to motels.

I got a job at a collection agency, but my credit was nearly as bad as my marriage. So I gave them a fake social security card. I would drink before work just to get through the day. The work was stressful—people would curse me out daily because the company focus was to call people who owed money and to pressure them into paying on old debts. I felt bad because I felt the same way they did. I could not pay my bills either! I met a lady on the job who was a little older than me with three kids. She always looks so sad and never really smiled. One day we were sitting at lunch and she asked if I knew anyone who would kill her husband. She was tired of him and wanted out, but she said it was impossible for her to leave he would find her. I was shocked that she asked me something like that. But I could see in her eyes that she was serious and desperate. I was looking at what my marital situation could have turned into.

Many relationships involving domestic violence end in someone killing, being killed, or being severely hurt. Many men and woman have gone to jail and lost their freedom trying to protect themselves from the abuse. I remember the lady from work telling me how abusive her husband was with her. She told me how he was well known in the city and that she could never get away from him with the three kids. She felt stuck and wanted him killed. I thought about how I may have been killed if I stayed with my abusive husband. When lunch ended we quickly got back to work. The next day I saw her again at lunch but we never spoke about our previous conversation. The following Friday I was called into the office and was told I was fired. They had found out about the fake social security number. I have never seen that lady again.

I wonder how many men and woman feel stuck in abusive relationships. There are usually early signs of abuse in relationships, yet we always think we can change someone. This way of thinking is dangerous. No one has the right to abuse you physically or mentally. If they do, it should be taken very seriously. If someone puts their hands on you once, they will most likely do it again. Moving on is the safest way—the only way. After I left my husband I never saw him again. I thought I would be happy after I left my husband and separated from my family, but I was wrong. I had a new family whose names were fear, hate, pain, guilt, anger, and shame. When you are full of hate, shame, and guilt, you start self-medicating and grow angry with the ones who you think caused the pain to begin with.

The cycle of guilt, anger, fear, and shame is at the heart of addiction. Now your soul is empty and longs to be filled with anything that numbs the pain. Regrets surface, and you find yourself just indulging in any quick fix whether it be food, sex, drugs, or gambling. It is so hard to find your way back. But you can find your way through forgiveness. I had to forgive my husband and the one who played a part in hurting me. I did not know how to forgive, because I could not forget. God told me to just start praying for my husband. I prayed for him to become a better man, a Godly man. I started to pray for my family. I continued to pray for God's mercy in my life. I noticed in time I started feeling happy again. The pain and anger were not there. I was more concerned about my well-being. I knew I had problems not only with addiction but with trust. I was thinking more clearly. I started going back to church and started serving. I knew God had forgiven me. Something had been lifted. I slept better and I started questioning my own behaviors in relationships. I knew I had a lot of work ahead in my recovery, but with God on my side I was no longer in fear of the idea of moving forward.

# Unforgiveness Is a Gateway That Only Hurts You

Do not hasten in your spirit to be angry,
For anger rests in the bosom of fools.
— Ecclesiastes 7:9, NKJV

It is so easy to continue to hold grudges against people who have done us wrong. We find it so hard to let it go. And that is understandable when someone has really hurt you, and the torment against you was devastating. We have every right to our feelings. Feelings do not lie, and they should never be ignored. Feelings are part of our inner being. When someone has deeply hurt us, we remember like it was yesterday. After I left my husband I held a grudge even over his name. I would not date another man who had the same name. Anyone with that name was bad. I did not know then that "unforgiveness" is poisonous. Just think about how many nights of sleep have you lost over someone who has hurt you. It's like a cancer eating away at us from the inside. It sucks up our energy and takes away our joy. Unforgiveness brings other negative emotions like anger, bitterness, blame, resentment, hostility, and hatred. Your health is in jeopardy because all these negative thoughts and emotions are bringing your body stress.

# Unforgiveness Causes Stress and Changes Our Behavior

Unforgiveness causes loss of appetite, anorexia, obesity, increased or excessive smoking or drinking of alcohol, anxiety, anger, depression, exhaustion, paranoia, and the feeling of being out of control. **Stress is linked to the six leading causes of death**—heart disease, cancer, lung ailments, accidents, cirrhosis of the liver, and suicide. Unforgiveness is a gateway to self-inflicted physical pain. Nine times out of ten, the ones who have hurt us have moved on, yet we are still living in the past. When we do not forgive someone, it is a stumbling block to our success. If we forgive others, we will be able to forgive ourselves and accept God's forgiveness. The biggest problem is figuring out how to forgive when the pain is too great. The good news is that we have God, and God asks that we pray for the ones who have hurt us. I prayed to God to help me to have a loving heart again, and I prayed for the people who hurt me. It was not easy at first, but it was worth it,  now I have joy and do not think about the pain anymore. I can share my painful past as a testimony that God listens and answers prayer. UN-forgiveness is a trap of Satan! We have to pray our way out!

"But I say unto you, Love your enemies, bless them that curse you, do good to them that hate you, and pray for them which despitefully use you, and persecute you," (*KJV*, Matthew 5:44)

For if you forgive men when they sin against you, your heavenly Father will
Also forgive you. But if you do not forgive men their sins, your Father will not forgive your
sins. (*NIV*, Matthew 6:14,15)

## Moving Forward

**Assignment:** Let's talk about the people that we have not forgiven. We learned the dangers of keeping unforgivness in our hearts, and how it can separate us from God's forgiveness. We know that the memories will remain, but the pain will go away once we start to pray. We can never control other people or what they do. However, we can control how long we will allow people to control us. It's our time to start moving forward.

**Action:** Make a list of the people who have done you harm. Pray for these people for forty days. Use your journal to help you keep track and document your prayers. Ask God to forgive you for not forgiving others. God will forgive you and this will also help you to forgive yourself.

1)_____

2)_____

3)_____

4)_____

5)_____

Journaling your thoughts and feelings helps you process events and release emotions. Journaling is a great tool for problem solving. Throughout this workbook you will find pages to journal your thoughts and dreams, and to document prayer requests and testimonials.

# JOURNAL

*Write down your thoughts and share them with the group.*

Date: _____

_____
_____
_____
_____
_____
_____
_____
_____
_____
_____
_____
_____
_____
_____
_____
_____
_____
_____
_____

For God speaks again and again, though people do not recognize it. He speaks in dreams, in visions of the night, when deep sleep falls on people as they lie in their beds. He whispers in their ears and terrifies them with warnings. He makes them turn from doing wrong; he keeps them from pride. He protects them from the grave, from crossing over the river of death. **(Job 33:14-18) (NLT)**

# DREAM JOURNAL

Day: _____                    Date: _____

Bedtime: _____                 Time Awake: _____

**Dream Details:**

_____

_____

_____

_____

_____

_____

_____

**Significance or Symbolism:**
_____

_____

_____

_____

# 4. Jesus Christ Our Lord And Savior

Jesus is the Son of God. He is God's only begotten son. He was conceived by the Holy Spirit, and born of a virgin. He lived in poverty, and He came from Nazareth. Even as a child, He was very knowledgeable. His knowledge came directly from God. Jesus was about thirty years of age at the start of his ministry, which began soon after his Baptism. Jesus chose twelve men to be his disciples. These men were everyday people who God used in an extraordinary way. The disciples had doubts, and struggles. They had faults like us and made mistakes. Some had bad attitudes and lost faith. But the disciples were radically changed following the death and resurrection of Jesus. They witnessed Jesus perform miracles healing sicknesses and diseases. He never used medicine; He fed thousands of people.

The demons knew who Jesus was, and they feared him. Jesus was a sin offering for the whole human race. People rejected Jesus. They could not believe this young man from Nazareth who was raised by Mary and Joseph was the Son of God. Jesus was known to have worked with his hands. He was the carpenter's son. Jesus was rejected and made fun of by men and woman. Even though He was innocent, He was condemned by Judges and sentenced to death on a cross because they did not believe He was the Son of God. By His suffering and death, He paid for the sins of all who believed in Him. He set us free. And we can only get to God through Jesus Christ in Jesus name, because of his sacrifice for mankind. Jesus saved us through his death and the shedding of his blood.

## Why did Jesus have to die for our sins?

Jesus died for our sins so we could have a relationship with God through eternity. We all have sinned against God. God's law comes with punishment, and the punishment is death and separation from God. Jesus was the only one who kept God's law. Even Satan himself tried to get Jesus to fall. Jesus maintained his integrity and responded by quoting the word of God to Satan, saying, "Again it is written, 'You shall not put the Lord, your God, to the test.'" Satan continued trying to deceive Jesus as he did Eve, even asking Jesus to worship him. Jesus continued to say, "Get away, Satan! It is written: 'The Lord, your God, shall you worship and him alone shall you serve,'"

"Then the devil left Him and, behold, angels came and ministered to Jesus.'"
**(Matthew 4) (KJV)** So Jesus was the perfect sacrifice; He had no sin and He was innocent. He died for us and our sins to save mankind. "For God so loved the world, that He gave his only begotten Son, that whosoever believes in Him should not perish, but have everlasting life," **(KJV, John 3:16)**

## We Are Reconciled To God Through The Blood Of Jesus

"Therefore, since we have been justified by faith, we have peace with God through our Lord Jesus Christ. Through him we have also obtained access by faith into this grace in which we stand, and we rejoice in the hope of the glory of God. Not only that, but we rejoice in our sufferings, knowing that suffering produces endurance, and endurance produces character, and character produces hope, and hope does not put us to shame, because God's love has been poured into our hearts through the Holy Spirit who has been given to us.

"For while we were still weak, at the right time Christ died for the ungodly. For one will scarcely die for a righteous person—though perhaps for a good person one would dare even to die—but God shows His love for us in that while we were still sinners, Christ died for us. Since, therefore, we have now been justified by His blood, much more shall we be saved by Him from the wrath of God. For if while we were enemies we were reconciled to God by the death of His Son, much more, now that we are reconciled, shall we be saved by His life. More than that, we also rejoice in God through our Lord Jesus Christ, through whom we have now received reconciliation," **(ESV, Romans 5:1-10)**

## Death Through Adam, Life Through Christ

"Therefore, just as sin came into the world through one man, and death through sin, and so death spread to all men because all sinned—for sin indeed was in the world before the law was given, but sin is not counted where there is no law. Yet death reigned from Adam to Moses, even over those whose sinning was not like the transgression of Adam, who was a type of the one who was to come.

"But the free gift is not like the trespass. For if many died through one man's trespass, much more have the grace of God and the free gift by the grace of that one man Jesus Christ abounded for many. And the free gift is not like the result of that one man's sin. For the judgment following one trespass brought condemnation, but the free gift following many trespasses brought justification. For if, because of one man's trespass, death reigned through that one man, much more will those who receive the abundance of grace and the free gift of righteousness reign in life through the one man Jesus Christ.

"Therefore, as one trespass led to condemnation for all men, so one act of righteousness leads to justification and life for all men. For as by the one man's disobedience the many were made sinners, so by the one man's obedience the many will be made righteous. Now the law came in to increase the trespass, but where sin increased, grace abounded all the more, so that, as sin reigned in death, grace also might reign through righteousness leading to eternal life through Jesus Christ our Lord,"
*(ESV, Roman 5:12-21)*

# The Testimony of Paul

Paul, then known as Saul, was a "zealous" Pharisee who "intensely persecuted" the followers of Jesus. However God chose to use Saul anyway. Let's read : You know what I was like when I followed the Jewish religion—how I violently persecuted God's church. I did my best to destroy it. [14] I was far ahead of my fellow Jews in my zeal for the traditions of my ancestors. **(Galatians 1:13-14) (NLT)**

What Paul is saying is before his conversion he truly believed in his heart that he was doing the right thing. He said he was following traditions. Saul persecuted Christians because he believed that anyone who believed in Jesus believed in a blasphemer. He thought that by persecuting them he was doing God's will. Many times we find ourselves following traditions or people that we look up to Saul did and he ended up being wrong. The book of Acts records that Paul was on his way from Jerusalem for Syrian Damascus to arrest followers of Jesus, with the intention of returning them to Jerusalem as prisoners for questioning and possible execution. The journey is interrupted when Paul sees a blinding light, and communicates directly with a divine voice. As he was approaching Damascus on this mission, a light from heaven suddenly shone down around him. [4] He fell to the ground and heard a voice saying to him, "Saul! Saul! Why are you persecuting me? "Who are you, lord?" Saul asked. And the voice replied, "I am Jesus, the one you are persecuting! [6] Now get up and go into the city, and you will be told what you must do." The men with Saul stood speechless, for they heard the sound of someone's voice but saw no one! [8] Saul picked himself up off the ground, but when he opened his eyes he was blind. So his companions led him by the hand to Damascus. [9] He remained there blind for three days and did not eat or drink. **( Acts 9:3-9 NLT)**

The account continues with a description of Ananias of Damascus receiving a divine revelation instructing him to visit Saul at the house of Judas on the Street Called Straight and there lay hands on him to restore his sight (the house of Judas is traditionally believed to have been near the west end of the street). Ananias is initially reluctant, having heard about Saul's persecution, but obeys the divine command: "But Lord," exclaimed Ananias, "I've heard many people talk about the terrible things this man has done to the believers in Jerusalem! [14] And he is authorized by the leading priests to arrest everyone who calls upon your name." But the Lord said, "Go, for Saul is my chosen instrument to take my message to the Gentiles and to kings, as well as to the people of Israel. [16] And I will show him how much he must suffer for my name's sake." So Ananias went and found Saul. He laid his hands on him and said, "Brother Saul, the Lord Jesus, who appeared to you on the road, has sent me so that you might regain your sight and be filled with the Holy Spirit." Instantly something like scales fell from Saul's eyes, and he regained his sight. Then he got up and was baptized. [19] Afterward he ate some food and regained his strength. **( Acts 9:13-19 NLT)**

The Conversion of Paul, in spite of his attempts to completely eradicate Christianity, is seen as evidence of God's Divine Grace. God does not care about your pass he cares about your future with him! You can read more of Pauls testimony in **(Acts 22)**

# Jesus Christ Our Lord And Savior

**Assignment:** I want to challenge you to read through the book of John it will help you come to a greater understanding of who Jesus Christ is  "So you might believe" Commit to 15 minutes a day and follow the reading schedule you will finish the book in a month. Put a check mark next to the day that you have finished reading until completed.

## 30  DAY READING PLAN

_____ Day 1.............................................................................................John 1:Who is Jesus

_____ Day 2.........................................................John 2:First Miracle/Cleansing of temple

_____ Day 3.............................................................................John 3:You must be born again

_____ Day 4............................................................................John 4: Jesus journeys in Samaria

_____ Day 5..............................................................................John 5: Jesus, the son of God

_____ Day6..............................................................................John 6:1-29: Feeding the 5000

_____ Day 7..........................................................................John 6:30-71: Jesus, the bread of life

_____ Day 8...........................................................................John 7: Jesus, teaching in the temple

_____ Day 9............................................................................John 8:Jesus,conflict with Pharisees

_____ Day 10................................................................................John 9: Healing the blind man

_____ Day 11................................................................John 10:1-21: Jesus, the good Shepherd

_____ Day 12...................................................................John 10:22-42 : Jesus is divine

_____ Day 13.........................................................John 11:Lazarus,raised from the dead

_____ Day 14............................................................................John 12:Jesus enters Jerusalem

_____ Day 15....................................................................................John 13:The Last Supper

_____ Day 16..........................................................John 14:1-14: Apostles receive comfort

_____ Day 17..........................................................John 14:15-31:Promise of the Holy Spirit

_____ Day 18................................................................................John 15:Abiding in Christ

_____ Day 19.........................................................John 16:1-15:Work of the Holy Spirit

_____ Day 20.........................................................John 16:16-33 :Jesus Prophesies

_____ Day 21...............................................................John 17: Jesus prays for followers

_____ Day 22............................................................................John 18:1-14 :Arrest of Jesus

_____ Day 23...........................................................John 18:15-27 :Peter denies Christ

_____ Day 24...........................................................John 18:28-40: Jesus before pilate

_____ Day 25...........................................................John 19:1-15: Jesus is condemned

_____ Day 26............................................................................John 19:16-30:The Crucifixion

_____ Day 27...........................................................John 19:31-42 : Jesus is buried

_____ Day 28.........................................................John 20:1-18 The resurrection

_____ Day 29..............................................................................John 20:19-31 Jesus appears

_____ Day 30...........................................................John 21: Events following the resurrection

Journaling your thoughts and feelings helps you process events and release emotions. Journaling is a great tool for problem solving. Throughout this workbook you will find pages to journal your thoughts and dreams, and to document prayer requests and testimonials.

# JOURNAL

*Write down your thoughts and share them with the group.*

Date: _____

_____
_____
_____
_____
_____
_____
_____
_____
_____
_____
_____
_____
_____
_____
_____
_____
_____
_____
_____
_____

# What Is Being A Disciple?

## The Great Commission

$^{16}$ Then the eleven disciples left for Galilee, going to the mountain where Jesus had told them to go. $^{17}$ When they saw him, they worshiped him—but some of them doubted!

$^{18}$ Jesus came and told his disciples, "I have been given all authority in heaven and on earth. $^{19}$ Therefore, go and make disciples of all the nations, baptizing them in the name of the Father and the Son and the Holy Spirit. $^{20}$ Teach these new disciples to obey all the commands I have given you. And be sure of this: I am with you always, even to the end of the age." **(Matthew 28:16-20) (NLT)**

A disciple is a student who follows a teacher. Jesus chose twelve disciples to follow Him. If you are a disciple, you should believe in the teacher you follow, and, in time, you should mirror their character. So a disciple's goal would be to become more Christ-like and to do as Jesus would. In order to be a successful disciple, you need the knowledge and the wisdom to carry out the task that you are given. You have to be taught. Jesus taught by example; He was a doer of the word. He never asked His disciples to do anything that He did not do Himself. It is the will of God for every believer to go out and let the truth of The Gospel of Jesus Christ be known.

Let's read what it says in Revelation: And they have defeated him by the blood of the Lamb and by their testimony. And they did not love their lives so much that they were afraid to die.
**(Revelation 12:11 NLT)**

Being a disciple means telling people about Jesus Christ and sharing the truth that God loved us so much He gave His only begotten son Jesus, who is the resurrection and the life.

Anyone who believes and obeys Jesus will live, even after physically dying. Disciples share how Jesus wants us to live by obeying His word and all that God commands. It means telling others how we have been blessed by following the word of God and sharing our testimony about how life has changed us for the better since we began following Jesus. The truth brings life to the lifeless. Knowing the truth about the Gospel of Jesus Christ provides protection from the Devil and his temptations.

Being a Christian, a believer of Jesus Christ, gives us access to the promise that God dwells in us and, through the Holy Spirit, gives us the knowledge of His kingdom. We have to stand in faith during tough times. Spending time with God and sharing the word of God will give us that inner peace and joy. God wants us to make disciples of all nations, baptizing them in the name of the Father and of the Son and of the Holy Spirit, teaching them to observe all that God has commanded.

## How to Be a Disciple:

1) **Love God with all your mind, heart, and soul:** When you truly love someone, you will do what pleases them. God should always be our first love, and we should go all out for Jesus.

"You shall love the Lord your God with all your heart, and with all your soul, and with all your strength, and with all your mind; and your neighbor as yourself," **(ESV, Luke 10:27)**

2) **Have unity to love one another:** When there is unity there is strength. When there is division, we fall.

"A new commandment I give to you, that you love one another: just as I have loved you, you also are to love one another. By this all people will know that you are my disciples, if you have love for one another," **(ESV, John 13:34-35)**

3) **Build everything on God:** Everything we do should always glorify God. Our jobs, ministries, and relationships should be in line with the word of God. When we are obedient to God, the promises come. God's word is sharper than a two-edged sword.

"Anyone who listens to my teaching and follows it is wise, like a person who builds a House on solid rock," **(NLT, Matthew 7:24)**

**4) Never take offense:** This does not mean you can never get your feelings hurt. God gives you inner joy that cannot be explained. Even in struggle, God provides Joy. Don't let others take this.

"Great peace have they which love thy law: and nothing shall offend them,"
**(KJV, Psalms 119:165)**

**5) Endure:** We have to have the endurance to get through pain and suffering, and to have the patience and courage to finish the race.

"Therefore, since we are surrounded by so great a cloud of witnesses, let us also lay aside every weight, and sin which clings so closely, and let us run with endurance the race that is set before us, looking to Jesus, the founder and perfecter of our faith, who for the joy that was set before Him endured the cross, despising the shame, and is seated at the right hand of the throne of God. Consider Him who endured from sinners such hostility against Himself, so that you may not grow weary or fainthearted,"
**(Hebrews 12:13) (ESV)**

**6) Pray:** Prayer is the way we communicate with God. We should never worry about anything, but pray about everything. God's promise is to be with us to the end of time. God loves us and knows what we need, even before we ask.

"After this manner therefore pray ye: Our Father which art in heaven, Hallowed be thy name. Thy kingdom come, Thy will be done in earth, as it is in heaven. Give us this day our daily bread. And forgive us our debts, as we forgive our debtors. And lead us not into temptation, but deliver us from evil: For thine is the kingdom, and the power, and the glory, forever. Amen."
**(KJV, Matthew 6:9-13)**

### The First Disciples

[16] One day as Jesus was walking along the shore of the Sea of Galilee, he saw Simon and his brother Andrew throwing a net into the water, for they fished for a living. [17] Jesus called out to them, "Come, follow me, and I will show you how to fish for people!" [18] And they left their nets at once and followed him. [19] A little farther up the shore Jesus saw Zebedee's sons, James and John, in a boat repairing their nets. [20] He called them at once, and they also followed him, leaving their father, Zebedee, in the boat with the hired men **(Mark 1:16-20) (NLT)**

# The Cost of Discipleship

Salvation is free but being a disciple comes with a cost, and Jesus made it clear that we need to count the cost if we truly want to be His disciple. To be a disciple you need to be obedient, devoted, and ready to carry your own cross. When the word says to carry your own cross, it means to surrender to God. One can only follow Christ by faith in what He has done for us at the cross, fully surrendering to God. We also have to be willing to give our time, talent, and treasures. Let's read a text about following Jesus:

## The Cost of Following Jesus

[18] When Jesus saw the crowd around him, he instructed his disciples to cross to the other side of the lake. [19] Then one of the teachers of religious law said to him, "Teacher, I will follow you wherever you go." [20] But Jesus replied, "Foxes have dens to live in, and birds have nests, but the Son of Man has no place even to lay his head." [21] Another of his disciples said, "Lord, first let me return home and bury my father." [22] But Jesus told him, "Follow me now. Let the spiritually dead bury their own dead." **(Matthew 8:18-22) (NLT)**

When we read the text, we see a teacher who was educated and impressed with Jesus. He said that he would follow Jesus wherever He would go. However, Jesus knows the heart of man. Many times we make decisions with the wrong motives and we have not even counted the cost of what it would take to follow Jesus. He told the teacher, "I do not even have a place to lay my head," which means Jesus had no possessions. Jesus told the rich young ruler in **Matthew 19:21** to sell everything he had and give to the poor, and he would have treasure in heaven and come and follow Him, but when the rich young ruler heard that saying, he went away sorrowful, for he had great possessions. Let's read another example in the following text about following Jesus:

**Luke 14:26 (NLT)** [26] "If you want to be my disciple, you must hate [love less] everyone else by comparison—your father and mother, wife and children, brothers and sisters—yes, even your own life. Otherwise, you cannot be my disciple."

This is a beautiful passage. Basically, you are completely sold to Jesus if you really know and love God. There can be no comparison to any earthly possessions or relationships, including family. And if you compared God to anything else, it would be to love everything else much less than God. The love we have for God cannot be measured. God is our rock, and we can't live without Him, but we can live without people and possessions. Amen!

We cannot have two objects of desire. Now, if your family is the object of your desire, then Jesus is not. So, when God says "hate," He is saying that the love for God has to be greater than your love for anyone else. That way, separation from PEOPLE AND THINGS will be more bearable because you are unattached to them and when it comes to following God, there will be nothing stopping you. That is why in the text God says to love much less (by comparison) even ourselves; we have to love God more than self. God will always come first. We cannot stop following God either, because who takes care of us? God! He will always take care of the ones who have faith and believe in Him. We have to know that everything we have belongs to God, and to be a disciple you have to trust God.

### Do not worry; to worry about self is the opposite of trusting God.

[25] "That is why I tell you not to worry about everyday life—whether you have enough food and drink, or enough clothes to wear. Isn't life more than food, and your body more than clothing? [26] Look at the birds. They don't plant or harvest or store food in barns, for your heavenly Father feeds them. And aren't you far more valuable to him than they are? [27] Can all your worries add a single moment to your life?

[28] "And why worry about your clothing? Look at the lilies of the field and how they grow. They don't work or make their clothing, [29] yet Solomon in all his glory was not dressed as beautifully as they are. [30] And if God cares so wonderfully for wildflowers that are here today and thrown into the fire tomorrow, he will certainly care for you. Why do you have so little faith?

[31] "So don't worry about these things, saying, 'What will we eat? What will we drink? What will we wear?' [32] These things dominate the thoughts of unbelievers, but **your heavenly Father already knows all your needs.** [33] **Seek the Kingdom of God above all else, and live righteously, and he will give you everything you need.**

[34] "So don't worry about tomorrow, for tomorrow will bring its own worries. Today's trouble is enough for today." **(Matthew 6:25-34) (NLT)**

Remember when another disciple said, "Lord, first let me return home and bury my father."[22] But Jesus told him, "Follow me now." God has to come first over EVERYTHING and everyone. If you love someone more than God then that person can also make you go against the will of God, so when it comes to God, you have to drop EVERYTHING and EVERYONE ELSE. If you are unwilling, then you cannot be His disciple. A disciple should never be ashamed either. I love the text that Paul wrote:

### Paul's Life for Christ

[20] According to my earnest expectation and my hope, that in nothing I shall be ashamed, but that with all boldness, as always, so now also Christ shall be magnified in my body, whether it be by life, or by death. [21] For to me to live is Christ, and to die is gain **(Philippians 1:20-21) (NLT)**

This is the attitude we should have as a disciple—to know the cost and to not be afraid of what can come. Paul is saying that if oppositions come, whether in life or death, he will not be ashamed because he knows the truth that Christ is life, and to die living by the word and for the word of God is gain. This is Paul's view and his desire to magnify the Lord by either his death or his life is being totally sold out to Jesus.

In Acts 5 Peter and the other apostles had been told not to teach in the name of Jesus, but Peter and the apostles replied, "We must obey God rather than any human authority. The God of our ancestors raised Jesus from the dead after you killed him by hanging him on a cross. Then God put him in the place of honor at his right hand as Prince and Savior. He did this so the people of Israel would repent of their sins and be forgiven. We are witnesses of these things and so is the Holy Spirit, who is given by God to those who obey him." When they heard this, the high council was furious and decided to kill them. But one member, a Pharisee named Gamaliel, who was an expert in religious law and respected by all the people, stood up and ordered that the men be sent outside the council chamber for a while. **(Acts 5:29-35) (NLT)**

Now, we see the boldness of the disciples and we also see the cost of telling the good news of Jesus Christ. The council was furious and wanted to kill them, but glory to God, they decided to let them go.

### Let's read what was done to the disciples and the warning that was given to them:

They called in the apostles and had them flogged (flogged is to be beaten severely with a whip or rod). Then, they ordered them never again to speak in the name of Jesus, and they let them go.

The disciples were put in jail, they were beaten, and their lives were threatened because they went out and made disciples of all nations, baptizing them in the name of the Father and of the Son and of the Holy Spirit, teaching people to obey everything God had commanded. The disciples could have quit anytime due to the cost of discipleship and the unbelievable beatings they took.

### Let's read the text of what the disciples' reaction was after the beatings and what they decided to do:

[41] The apostles left the high council rejoicing that God had counted them worthy to suffer disgrace for the name of Jesus. [42] And every day, in the Temple and from house to house, they continued to teach and preach this message: "Jesus is the Messiah." **(Acts 5:41) (NLT)**

Can you imagine? After all they had been through they rejoiced and they continued to teach and preach this message: "Jesus is the Messiah," because they understood the cost and the value of eternity, which is everlasting life with Christ, but without Christ it is death. Once again we must read the word of God and understand the cost of being a disciple so that we know what it will take to finish the race!

### For the ones who follow come great rewards:

[29] "Yes," Jesus replied, "and I assure you that everyone who has given up house or brothers or sisters or mother or father or children or property, for my sake and for the Good News, [30] will receive now in return a hundred times as many houses, brothers, sisters, mothers, children, and property—along with persecution. And in the world to come that person will have eternal life." **(Mark 10:29-30) (NLT)**

We are all called out to be disciples of Jesus Christ, if we are true Christians. We must count the cost and know that we have to be obedient to God's word and stay committed in our walk. We must be loving and kind to others and willing to serve them. We model after Jesus, and if you are willing, don't worry about your education, current position, etc. If you love the Lord and believe in God, pray, trust and obey God, He will use you in a mighty way. The Holy Spirit, who is God, will guide you by His Word. We just have to understand the cost because there is opposition and God prepares His people, so when they learn the cost of being a disciple, they can brush themselves off after every battle and struggle and know that God counted them worthy to suffer disgrace for the name of Jesus! So, never quit. God has you and is always with you, even to the end of the age. AMEN!!

"Therefore, go and make disciples of all the nations, baptizing them in the name of the Father and the Son and the Holy Spirit. [20] Teach these new disciples to obey all the commands I have given you. And be sure of this: I am with you always, even to the end of the age." **(Matthew 28:19-20) (NLT)**

## Bible Verses about Disciples

[31] Jesus said to the people who believed in him, "You are truly my disciples if you remain faithful to my teachings. [32] And you will know the truth, and the truth will set you free. [33] But we are descendants of Abraham," they said. "We have never been slaves to anyone. What do you mean, 'You will be set free'? [34] Jesus replied, "I tell you the truth, everyone who sins is a slave of sin. [35] A slave is not a permanent member of the family, but a son is part of the family forever. [36] So if the Son sets you free, you are truly free. **[John 8:31-36]**

"I tell you the truth, anyone who believes in me will do the same works I have done, and even greater works, because I am going to be with the Father. **[John 14:12]**

10 Jesus called his twelve disciples together and gave them authority to cast out evil spirits and to heal every kind of disease and illness. **[Mathew 10:1]**

[19] When you are arrested, don't worry about how to respond or what to say. God will give you the right words at the right time. [20] For it is not you who will be speaking—it will be the Spirit of your Father speaking through you. **[Mathew 10:19-20]**

"Behold, I send you forth as sheep in the midst of wolves: Be ye therefore wise as serpents, and harmless as doves." **[Matthew 10:16, KJV]**

[8] Then Peter, filled with the Holy Spirit, said to them, "Rulers and elders of our people, [9] are we being questioned today because we've done a good deed for a crippled man? Do you want to know how he was healed? [10] Let me clearly state to all of you and to all the people of Israel that he was healed by the powerful name of Jesus Christ the Nazarene, the man you crucified but whom God raised from the dead. [11] For Jesus is the one referred to in the Scriptures, where it says,

'The stone that you builders rejected
    has now become the cornerstone.'

[12] There is salvation in no one else! God has given no other name under heaven by which we must be saved." **[Act 4:8-12]**

[66] At this point many of his disciples turned away and deserted him. [67] Then Jesus turned to the Twelve and asked, "Are you also going to leave?"

[68] Simon Peter replied, "Lord, to whom would we go? You have the words that give eternal life. [69] We believe, and we know you are the Holy One of God.]" **[John 6:66-69]**

[11] Now these are the gifts Christ gave to the church: the apostles, the prophets, the evangelists, and the pastors and teachers. [12] Their responsibility is to equip God's people to do his work and build up the church, the body of Christ. **[Ephesians 4:11-12]**

### We Are God's Ambassadors

[11] Because we understand our fearful responsibility to the Lord, we work hard to persuade others. God knows we are sincere, and I hope you know this, too. [12] Are we commending ourselves to you again? No, we are giving you a reason to be proud of us, so you can answer those who brag about having a spectacular ministry rather than having a sincere heart. [13] If it seems we are crazy, it is to bring glory to God. And if we are in our right minds, it is for your benefit. [14] Either way, Christ's love controls us. Since we believe that Christ died for all, we also believe that we have all died to our old life. [15] He died for everyone so that those who receive his new life will no longer live for themselves. Instead, they will live for Christ, who died and was raised for them.

[16] So we have stopped evaluating others from a human point of view. At one time we thought of Christ merely from a human point of view. How differently we know him now! [17] This means that anyone who belongs to Christ has become a new person. The old life is gone; a new life has begun!

[18] And all of this is a gift from God, who brought us back to himself through Christ. And God has given us this task of reconciling people to him. [19] For God was in Christ, reconciling the world to himself, no longer counting people's sins against them. And he gave us this wonderful message of reconciliation. [20] So we are Christ's ambassadors; God is making his appeal through us. We speak for Christ when we plead, "Come back to God!" [21] For God made Christ, who never sinned, to be the offering for our sin, so that we could be made right with God through Christ. 6 As God's partners, we beg you not to accept this marvelous gift of God's kindness and then ignore it. [2] For God says,"At just the right time, I heard you.
    On the day of salvation, I helped you."Indeed, the "right time" is now. Today is the day of salvation.
**[2 Corinthians 5:11]**

" Therefore, go and make disciples of all the nations, baptizing them in the name of the Father and the Son and the Holy Spirit. [20] Teach these new disciples to obey all the commands I have given you. And be sure of this: I am with you always, even to the end of the age."(MATTHEW 28:19-20) (NLT)

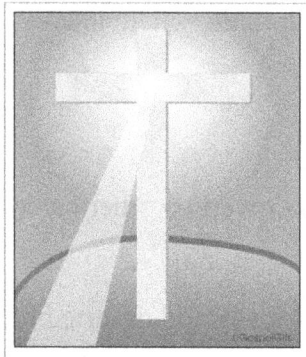

## How to Be a Disciple

**Assignment:** Why do you think God would want you to be a disciple, and to then go out and make disciples? Journal your thoughts.

**Action:** What is stopping you from being a disciple, Will you become a follower of Jesus? Journal your thoughts.

1)_____

2)_____

3)_____

4)_____

5)_____

Journaling your thoughts and feelings helps you process events and release emotions. Journaling is a great tool for problem solving. Throughout this workbook you will find pages to journal your thoughts and dreams, and to document prayer requests and testimonials.

# JOURNAL

*Write down your thoughts and share them with the group.*

Date: _____

_____

_____

_____

_____

_____

_____

_____

_____

_____

_____

_____

_____

_____

_____

_____

_____

_____

_____

# What is Baptism?

"And Jesus came and said to them, 'All authority in heaven and on earth has been given to me. Go therefore and make disciples of all nations, baptizing them in the name of the Father and of the Son and of the Holy Spirit, teaching them to observe all that I have commanded you. And behold, I am with you always, to the end of the age.'"

Being baptized is a public announcement that you are a sinner and that you repent for your sins against God. We all sin against God because of our mindset and our heart. Jesus said that we cannot see the Kingdom unless we are born again. We have to have a change of heart and a transformation. When we get baptized, we are symbolically turning from our rebellious ways. It means that we place our faith in Jesus Christ and believe in the gospel—that Jesus lived a life of perfect righteousness, of perfect obedience, and that He was crucified and died on the cross for our sins. We know that Jesus rose on the third day to live again. We, too, want to be reborn and follow God's commands to enter His Kingdom.

1) Being baptized means saying you have had a change of heart and believing in Christ enough to repent of your sin. Repenting means you have knowledge that you sinned against God, and that you regret sinning. You want to change the direction of your life to follow Jesus.

2) The second command is to be baptized into Christ. This means that you are surrendering yourself, identifying yourself completely with Jesus as your Lord and Savior.

The first promise of baptism is that you will receive the forgiveness of your sins. Everything you've done wrong, every sin you've ever committed, will be washed completely away. The second promise is that you will receive the gift of the Holy Spirit. That is, you'll be empowered by the Spirit of God to live this life of following Christ.

In **Acts 2:41**; those who accepted Christ's message were, in fact, baptized. Three thousand of them were baptized on that Day of Pentecost.

God also tells us that He will be with us forever. Amen to that! God gives us the good news by telling us, "Therefore, if anyone *is* in Christ, *he is* a new creation; old things have passed away; behold, all things have become new," **(NKJV, 2 Corinthians 5:17)**

God said all things have passed away, and you are a new creation. So no more looking back, and no more guilt. From this day forward, when you do something wrong against God, quickly apologize and tell God you are sorry. God knows we are not perfect, and He forgives.

## You Must Be Born Again

"There was a man named Nicodemus, a Jewish religious leader who was a Pharisee. [2] After dark one evening, he came to speak with Jesus. "Rabbi," he said, "we all know that God has sent you to teach us. Your miraculous signs are evidence that God is with you."

[3] Jesus replied, "I tell you the truth, unless you are born again, you cannot see the Kingdom of God."

[4] "What do you mean?" exclaimed Nicodemus. "How can an old man go back into his mother's womb and be born again?"

[5] Jesus replied, "I assure you, no one can enter the Kingdom of God without being born of water and the Spirit. [6] Humans can reproduce only human life, but the Holy Spirit gives birth to spiritual life. [7] So don't be surprised when I say, 'You must be born again.' [8] The wind blows wherever it wants. Just as you can hear the wind but can't tell where it comes from or where it is going, so you can't explain how people are born of the Spirit."

[9] "How are these things possible?" Nicodemus asked. [10] Jesus replied, "You are a respected Jewish teacher, and yet you don't understand these things? [11] I assure you, we tell you what we know and have seen, and yet you won't believe our testimony. [12] But if you don't believe me when I tell you about earthly things, how can you possibly believe if I tell you about heavenly things? [13] No one has ever gone to heaven and returned. But the Son of Man has come down from heaven. [14] And as Moses lifted up the bronze snake on a pole in the wilderness, so the Son of Man must be lifted up, [15] so that everyone who believes in him will have eternal life." **(John 3:1-15) (NLT)**

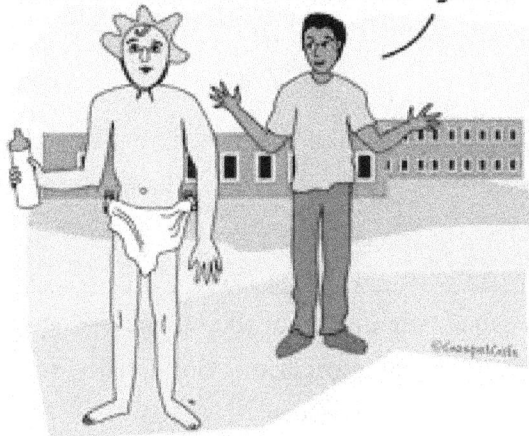

Charles, I doubt that's what Jesus meant when He said we must be born again...

# Philip and the Ethiopian Eunuch

"Now an angel of the Lord said to Philip, 'Rise and go toward the south to the road that goes down from Jerusalem to Gaza.' This is a desert place. And he rose and went. And there was an Ethiopian, a eunuch, a court official of Candace, queen of the Ethiopians, who was in charge of all her treasure. He had come to Jerusalem to worship and was returning, seated in his chariot, and he was reading the prophet Isaiah. And the Spirit said to Philip, 'Go over and join this chariot.' So Philip ran to him and heard him reading Isaiah the prophet and asked, 'Do you understand what you are reading?' And he said, 'How can I, unless someone guides me?' And he invited Philip to come up and sit with him. Now the passage of the Scripture that he was reading was this:

'Like a sheep he was led to the slaughter
and like a lamb before its shearer is silent,
so he opens not his mouth.
In his humiliation justice was denied him.
Who can describe his generation?
For his life is taken away from the earth.'

"And the eunuch said to Philip, 'About whom, I ask you, does the prophet say this, about himself or about someone else?' Then Philip opened his mouth, and beginning with this Scripture he told him the good news about Jesus. And as they were going along the road they came to some water, and the eunuch said, "See, here is water! What prevents me from being baptized?' And he commanded the chariot to stop, and they both went down into the water, Philip and the eunuch, and he baptized him. And when they came up out of the water, the Spirit of the Lord carried Philip away, and the eunuch saw him no more, and went on his way rejoicing," **(ESV, Acts 8:26-40)**

## The Baptism of Jesus

"Then Jesus went from Galilee to the Jordan River to be baptized by John. But John tried to talk him out of it. 'I am the one who needs to be baptized by you,' he said, 'so why are you coming to me?'

"But Jesus said, 'It should be done, for we must carry out all that God requires.' So John agreed to baptize him."After his baptism, as Jesus came up out of the water, the heavens were opened and He saw the Spirit of God descending like a dove and settling on Him. And a voice from heaven said, 'This is my dearly loved Son, who brings me great joy,'" **(NLT, Matthew 3:13-17)**

# Gentiles Hear the Good News

"So Peter opened his mouth and said: 'Truly I understand that God shows no partiality, but in every nation anyone who fears Him and does what is right is acceptable to Him. As for the word that He sent to Israel, preaching good news of peace through Jesus Christ (He is Lord of all), you yourselves know what happened throughout all Judea, beginning from Galilee after the baptism that John proclaimed: how God anointed Jesus of Nazareth with the Holy Spirit and with power. He went about doing good and healing all who were oppressed by the devil, for God was with Him. And we are witnesses of all that He did both in the country of the Jews and in Jerusalem. They put Him to death by hanging Him on a tree, but God raised Him on the third day and made Him to appear, not to all the people but to us who had been chosen by God as witnesses, who ate and drank with Him after he rose from the dead. And He commanded us to preach to the people and to testify that He is the one appointed by God to be judge of the living and the dead. To Him all the prophets bear witness that everyone who believes in Him receives forgiveness of sins through His name," **(ESV, Acts 10:34-43)**

## The Holy Spirit Falls on the Gentiles

"While Peter was still saying these things, the Holy Spirit fell on all who heard the word. And the believers from among the circumcised who had come with Peter were amazed, because the gift of the Holy Spirit was poured out even on the Gentiles. For they were hearing them speaking in tongues and extolling God. Then Peter declared, 'Can anyone withhold water for baptizing these people, who have received the Holy Spirit just as we have?' And he commanded them to be baptized in the name of Jesus Christ. Then they asked him to remain for some days," **(ESV, Acts 10:44-48)**

## The Coming of the Holy Spirit (ACTS 2) (NKJV)

"When the day of Pentecost arrived, they were all together in one place. And suddenly there came from heaven a sound like a mighty rushing wind, and it filled the entire house where they were sitting. And divided tongues as of fire appeared to them and rested on each one of them. And they were all filled with the Holy Spirit and began to speak in other tongues as the Spirit gave them utterance.

"Now there were dwelling in Jerusalem Jews, devout men from every nation under heaven. And at this sound the multitude came together, and they were bewildered, because each one was hearing them speak in his own language. And they were amazed and astonished, saying, 'Are not all these who are speaking Galileans? And how is it that we hear, each of us in his own native language? Parthians and Medes and Elamites and residents of Mesopotamia, Judea and Cappadocia, Pontus and Asia, Phrygia and Pamphylia, Egypt and the parts of Libya belonging to Cyrene, and visitors from Rome, both

Jews and proselytes, Cretans and Arabians—we hear them telling in our own tongues the mighty works of God.' And all were amazed and perplexed, saying to one another, 'What does this mean?' But others mocking said, 'They are filled with new wine,'" **(NKJV, Acts 2:1-13)**

## Peter's Sermon

"But Peter, standing up with the eleven, raised his voice and said to them, 'Men of Judea and all who dwell in Jerusalem, let this be known to you, and heed my words. For these are not drunk, as you suppose, since it is *only* the third hour of the day. But this is what was spoken by the prophet Joel:

'And it shall come to pass in the last days, says God,

That I will pour out of My Spirit on all flesh;

Your sons and your daughters shall prophesy,

Your young men shall see visions,

Your old men shall dream dreams.

And on My menservants and on My maidservants

I will pour out My Spirit in those days;

And they shall prophesy.

I will show wonders in heaven above

And signs in the earth beneath:

Blood and fire and vapor of smoke.

The sun shall be turned into darkness,

And the moon into blood,

Before the coming of the great and awesome day of the LORD.

And it shall come to pass

*That* whoever calls on the name of the LORD

Shall be saved.'

"'Men of Israel, hear these words: Jesus of Nazareth, a Man attested by God to you by miracles, wonders, and signs which God did through Him in your midst, as you yourselves also know— Him, being delivered by the determined purpose and foreknowledge of God, you have taken by lawless hands, have crucified, and put to death; whom God raised up, having loosed the pains of death, because it was not possible that He should be held by it. For David says concerning Him:

'I foresaw the LORD always before my face,

For He is at my right hand, that I may not be shaken.

Therefore my heart rejoiced, and my tongue was glad;

Moreover my flesh also will rest in hope.

For You will not leave my soul in Hades,

Nor will You allow Your Holy One to see corruption.

You have made known to me the ways of life;

You will make me full of joy in Your presence.'


"'Men *and* brethren, let *me* speak freely to you of the patriarch David, that he is both dead and buried, and his tomb is with us to this day. Therefore, being a prophet, and knowing that God had sworn with an oath to him that of the fruit of his body, according to the flesh, He would raise up the Christ to sit on his throne, he, foreseeing this, spoke concerning the resurrection of the Christ, that His soul was not left in Hades, nor did His flesh see corruption. This Jesus God has raised up, of which we are all witnesses. Therefore being exalted to the right hand of God, and having received from the Father the promise of the Holy Spirit, He poured out this which you now see and hear.

"For David did not ascend into the heavens, but he says himself:

'The LORD said to my Lord,

Sit at My right hand,

Till I make Your enemies Your footstool.'

"Therefore let all the house of Israel know assuredly that God has made this Jesus, whom you crucified, both Lord and Christ."

"Now when they heard this, they were cut to the heart, and said to Peter and the rest of the apostles, 'Men and brethren, what shall we do?'

"Then Peter said to them, 'Repent, and let every one of you be baptized in the name of Jesus Christ for the remission of sins; and you shall receive the gift of the Holy Spirit. For the promise is to you and to your children, and to all who are afar off, as many as the Lord our God will call,'"

Now the eleven disciples went to Galilee, to the mountain to which Jesus had directed them. And when they saw Him they worshiped Him, but some doubted. And Jesus came and said to them, "All authority in heaven and on earth has been given to me. Go therefore and make disciples of all nations, baptizing them in the name of the Father and of the Son and of the Holy Spirit, teaching them to observe all that I have commanded you. And behold, I am with you always, to the end of the age," **(ESV, Matthew 28:18-20)**

# Bible Verses about Baptism

Do you not know that all of us who have been baptized into Christ Jesus were baptized into his death? We were buried therefore with him by baptism into death, in order that, just as Christ was raised from the dead by the glory of the Father, we too might walk in newness of life."
**[Romans 6:3]**

"One Lord, one faith, one baptism"
**[Ephesians 4:5]**

"John appeared, baptizing in the wilderness and proclaiming a baptism of repentance for the forgiveness of sins."
**[Mark 1:4]**

"I baptize you with water for repentance, but he who is coming after me is mightier than I, whose sandals I am not worthy to carry. He will baptize you with the Holy Spirit and fire."
**[Matthew 3:11]**

When he died, he died once to break the power of sin. But now that he lives, he lives for the glory of God. So you also should consider yourselves to be dead to the power of sin and alive to God through Christ Jesus. Do not let sin control the way you live; do not give in to sinful desires. Do not let any part of your body become an instrument of evil to serve sin. Instead, give yourselves completely to God, for you were dead, but now you have new life. So use your whole body as an instrument to do what is right for the glory of God.
**[Romans 6:10-13]**

And Peter said to them, Repent and be baptized every one of you in the name of Jesus Christ for the forgiveness of your sins, and you will receive the gift of the Holy Spirit."
**[Acts 2:38]**

When you came to Christ, you were "circumcised," but not by a physical procedure. Christ performed a spiritual circumcision—the cutting away of your sinful nature. For you were buried with Christ when you were baptized. And with him you were raised to new life because you trusted the mighty power of God, who raised Christ from the dead..
**[Colossians 2:11-12]**

And this water symbolizes baptism that now saves you also—not the removal of dirt from the body but the pledge of a clear conscience toward God. It saves you by the resurrection of Jesus Christ,
**[1 peter 3:21]**

## Jesus said to observe all that I have commanded you

But don't just listen to God's word. You must do what it says. Otherwise, you are only fooling yourselves. For if you listen to the word and don't obey, it is like glancing at your face in a mirror. You see yourself, walk away, and forget what you look like. But if you look carefully into the perfect law that sets you free, and if you do what it says and don't forget what you heard, then God will bless you for doing it.
**(James 1:22-25) (NLT)**

## True Wisdom Comes from God

If you are wise and understand God's ways, prove it by living an honorable life, doing good works with the humility that comes from wisdom. But if you are bitterly jealous and there is selfish ambition in your heart, don't cover up the truth with boasting and lying. For jealousy and selfishness are not God's kind of wisdom. Such things are earthly, unspiritual, and demonic. For wherever there is jealousy and selfish ambition, there you will find disorder and evil of every kind. **(James 3:13-16) (NLT)**

---

### Jesus Christ Our Lord And Savior

**Assignment:** Why do you have to be baptized? Journal your thoughts.

"But Jesus said, 'It should be done, for we must carry out all that God requires.' So John agreed to baptize him. **(Matthew 3:15 NIV)**

"And now why do you wait? Rise and be baptized and wash away your sins, calling on the name of the Lord." **(Acts 22:16)**

**Action:** If you have not been baptized and God requires it, what is stopping you from being baptized?

1)_____

2)_____

3)_____

4)_____

5)_____

---

Journaling your thoughts and feelings helps you process events and release emotions. Journaling is a great tool for problem solving. Throughout this workbook you will find pages to journal your thoughts and dreams, and to document prayer requests and testimonials.

# JOURNAL

*Write down your thoughts and share them with the group.*

Date: _____

---

---

---

---

---

---

---

---

---

---

---

---

---

---

---

---

---

---

---

---

> For God speaks again and again, though people do not recognize it. He speaks in dreams, in visions of the night, when deep sleep falls on people as they lie in their beds. He whispers in their ears and terrifies them with warnings. He makes them turn from doing wrong; he keeps them from pride. He protects them from the grave, from crossing over the river of death. **(Job 33:14-18) (NLT)**

# DREAM JOURNAL

Day: _____          Date: _____

Bedtime: _____          Time Awake: _____

**Dream Details:**

_____

_____

_____

_____

_____

_____

_____

**Significance or Symbolism:**

_____

_____

_____

_____

# 5. The Holy Spirit

**The Holy Spirit is called God**: The Holy Spirit is the divine. The Holy Spirit is God. Peter made it clear that the Holy Spirit is God Himself in Acts when he said, "Ananias, why have you let Satan fill your heart? You lied to the Holy Spirit, and you kept some of the money for yourself. The property was yours to sell or not sell, as you wished. And after selling it, the money was also yours to give away. How could you do a thing like this? You weren't lying to us but to God!" **(NLT, Acts 5:3-4)**

**The Holy Spirit is all-powerful:** When Mary was told by the Angel Gabriel that she would conceive and give birth to a son, whom she would name Jesus, Mary was shocked, asking the angel how this could happen if she was a virgin. The Angel replied, "The Holy Spirit will come upon you, and the power of the Most High will overshadow you. So the baby to be born will be holy, and he will be called the Son of God," **(NLT, Luke 1:35)** When we read the text, we can see the Trinity—The Father, The Son, and The Holy Spirit—working together.

**He is the creator:** The first biblical text about the Holy Spirit can be found in Genesis when the Spirit of God hovers over the waters. Genesis 1:1 says that; In the beginning, God created the heavens and the earth.

**The Father, The Son, and The Holy Spirit are one**: "And God said, Let us make man in our image, after our likeness," **(KJV, Genesis 1:26)** God said let "us " when He created Adam, and when Adam and Eve ate of the forbidden fruit, God said, "Behold, the man is become as one of us to know good and evil" **(KJV, Genesis 3:22)** again making it clear that The Father, The Son, and The Holy Spirit was one from the beginning.

**The Holy Spirit is the third person in the God-head.** "For there are three that bear witness in heaven: the Father, the Word, and the Holy Spirit; and these three are one," **(NKJV, 1 John 5:7)**

**The Holy Spirit is the promise of the Father:** "And I will ask the Father, and He will give you another Advocate, who will never leave you. He is the Holy Spirit, who leads into all truth. The world cannot receive Him, because it isn't looking for Him and doesn't recognize Him. But you know Him, because He lives with you now and later will be in you," **(NLT, John 14:16)**

**Salvation revives God's spirit within us:** "So I want you to know that no one speaking by the Spirit of God will curse Jesus, and no one can say Jesus is Lord, except by the Holy Spirit," **(NLT, 1Corinthians 12:3)**

**The Holy Spirit is responsible for gifts of the spirit:** "There are different kinds of spiritual gifts, but the same Spirit is the source of them all" **(NLT, 1Corinthians 12:4)** "A spiritual gift is given to each of us so we can help each other," **( NLT, 1Corinthians 12:7)**

**Will we all speak in tongues once the Holy Spirit fills us?** "As soon as they heard this, they were baptized in the name of the Lord Jesus. Then when Paul laid his hands on them, the Holy Spirit came on them, and they spoke in other tongues and prophesied. There were about twelve men in all." **(Acts 19:5-7)**

Speaking in tongues is a gift of the Holy Spirit, not evidence of the Holy Spirit. A spiritual gift is given to each of us so we can help each other. To one person the Spirit gives the ability to give wise advice; to another the same Spirit gives a message of special knowledge. The same Spirit gives great faith to another, and to someone else the one Spirit gives the gift of healing. He gives one person the power to perform miracles, and another the ability to prophesy. He gives someone else the ability to discern whether a message is from the Spirit of God or from another spirit. Still another person is given the ability to speak in unknown languages, while another is given the ability to interpret what is being said. It is the one and only Spirit who distributes all these gifts. He alone decides which gift each person should have, **(NLT, 1 Corinthians 12:7-11)**

## What then is the evidence of the Holy Spirit in your life?

"I say then: Walk in the Spirit, and you shall not fulfill the lust of the flesh. For the flesh lusts against the Spirit, and the Spirit against the flesh; and these are contrary to one another, so that you do not do the things that you wish. But if you are led by the Spirit, you are not under the law.

"Now the works of the flesh are evident, which are: adultery, fornication, uncleanness, lewdness, idolatry, sorcery, hatred, contentions, jealousies, outbursts of wrath, selfish ambitions, dissensions, heresies, envy, murders, drunkenness, revelries, and the like; of which I tell you beforehand, just as I also told *you* in time past, that those who practice such things will not inherit the kingdom of God.

"But the fruit of the Spirit is love, joy, peace, long-suffering, kindness, goodness, faithfulness, gentleness, self-control. Against such there is no law. And those *who are* Christ's have crucified the flesh with its passions and desires. If we live in the Spirit, let us also walk in the Spirit. Let us not become conceited, provoking one another, envying one another," **(NLT, Galatians 5:16-26)**

**Blaspheming the Holy Spirit:** "So I tell you, every sin and blasphemy can be forgiven—except blasphemy against the Holy Spirit, which will never be forgiven. Anyone who speaks against the Son of Man can be forgiven, but anyone who speaks against the Holy Spirit will never be forgiven, either in this world or in the world to come," **(NLT, Matthew 12:31-32)**

## Example of Blaspheming the Holy Spirit in Mark 3:20-30 Let's read:

### Jesus and the Prince of Demons

[20] One time Jesus entered a house, and the crowds began to gather again. Soon he and his disciples couldn't even find time to eat. [21] When his family heard what was happening, they tried to take him away. "He's out of his mind," they said.

[22] But the teachers of religious law who had arrived from Jerusalem said, "He's possessed by Satan, the prince of demons. That's where he gets the power to cast out demons."

[23] Jesus called them over and responded with an illustration. "How can Satan cast out Satan?" he asked. [24] "A kingdom divided by civil war will collapse. [25] Similarly, a family splintered by feuding will fall apart. [26] And if Satan is divided and fights against himself, how can he stand? He would never survive. [27] Let me illustrate this further. Who is powerful enough to enter the house of a strong man like Satan and plunder his goods? Only someone even stronger—someone who could tie him up and then plunder his house.

[28] "I tell you the truth, all sin and blasphemy can be forgiven, [29] but anyone who blasphemes the Holy Spirit will never be forgiven. This is a sin with eternal consequences." [30] He told them this because they were saying, "He's possessed by an evil spirit."

The fool has said in his heart, "There is no God."
— Psalm 53:1

**Other name's of the Holy Spirit:** Holy Ghost, The spirit of God, Comforter, Advocate

## The Work of the Holy Spirit

[5] "But now I am going away to the one who sent me, and not one of you is asking where I am going. [6] Instead, you grieve because of what I've told you. [7] But in fact, it is best for you that I go away, because if I don't, the Advocate won't come. If I do go away, then I will send him to you. [8] And when he comes, he will convict the world of its sin, and of God's righteousness, and of the coming judgment. [9] The world's sin is that it refuses to believe in me. [10] Righteousness is available because I go to the Father, and you will see me no more. [11] Judgment will come because the ruler of this world has already been judged. [12] "There is so much more I want to tell you, but you can't bear it now. [13] When the Spirit of truth comes, he will guide you into all truth. He will not speak on his own but will tell you what he has heard. He will tell you about the future. [14] He will bring me glory by telling you whatever he receives from me. [15] All that belongs to the Father is mine; this is why I said, 'The Spirit will tell you whatever he receives from me.'**(John 16) (NLT)**

The work of the Holy Spirit teaches us and reminds us of the word of God. He convicts us of sin and guides us into truth. The Holy Spirit helps us pray and He transforms the follower and produces Christ like traits in us. All the gifts of the spirit are given to help the church. All gifts and abilities come from God. Some of us will have the same gift and some of us will not. God decides the gifts each one of us will have. We are designed to depend on the Holy Spirit because He is all knowing (God). The Holy Spirit is full of power.

At that moment the Spirit of the LORD came powerfully upon him, and he ripped the lion's jaws apart with his bare hands. He did it as easily as if it was a young goat. But he didn't tell his father or mother about it. **(Judges 14:6) 9NLT)**

A lot of us operate in our gifts naturally. We need to embrace these gifts and not misuse them. We can grieve the Holy Spirit by our behavior and the way we live.

And do not bring sorrow to God's Holy Spirit by the way you live. Remember, he has identified you as his own, guaranteeing that you will be saved on the day of redemption. **(Ephesians 4:30) (NLT)**

# How To Be Filled With The Holy Spirit

The first thing to know and understand is that God commands us to be filled with the Holy Spirit. At the same time, God gives us free will. If we do not ask to be filled, it is our fault entirely. Once we receive Jesus Christ into our lives, the Holy Spirit comes to dwell within us. The new believer will sometimes think once they have received Jesus Christ, and once the Holy Spirit dwells within them, they will not sin any longer. They are then surprised that they are still sinners. Before we accept Jesus Christ, there is only one force at work in us—carnal nature. When we receive Jesus Christ and the Holy Spirit dwells within us, then there are two natures at work—our old sinful nature that lives for self, and the new spiritual nature that wants to live for God. This is why God promises the gift of the Holy Spirit when we receive Jesus Christ. Unless the Holy Spirit rules over our lives, we will be dominated by our sinful nature. Just like the rich man who asked Jesus what must he do to inherit eternal life, Jesus tells us to follow his commandments. The rich man argued that he had always followed Jesus' commandments since he was a boy. Jesus responded that he still lacked one thing. Sell everything you have, Jesus said, and give to the poor, and then you will have treasure in heaven. Then come, follow me. When the rich man heard this, he became very sad, because he was a man of great wealth. In this example, God is offering the rich man the Kingdom of Heaven, but because the man is led by his carnal sinful nature, he cannot see that what Jesus is offering is much greater than his earthly wealth. The man confessed his guilt before God and would not submit to the Lordship of Christ, because of his desire for wealth.

**How do we become filled with the Holy Spirit:** The Holy Spirit is a gift given to all believers in Jesus without exception, and no conditions are placed upon this gift except faith in Christ.

## Rivers of Living Water

"Now on the last day, the great *day* of the feast, Jesus stood and cried out, saying, 'If anyone is thirsty, let him come to Me and drink. He who believes in Me, as the Scripture said, 'From his innermost being will flow rivers of living water.'' But this He spoke of the Spirit, whom those who believed in Him were to receive; for the Spirit was not yet *given*, because Jesus was not yet glorified,"
**(NASB, John 7:37-39)**

The Holy Spirit produces the fruit of the Spirit, which is "love, joy, peace, long-suffering, kindness, goodness, faithfulness, gentleness, self-control," **(Galatians 5:22-23)** Possessing the fruit of the spirit is what helps us to serve others rather than ourselves. It also teaches us to love the way God wants us to love. The power of the Holy Spirit gives us the power to serve Jesus. The Bible says: "The Holy Spirit helps when we are powerless. Likewise the Spirit helps us in our weakness. Since we do not know what to pray for as we ought, but the Spirit himself intercedes for us with groans too deep for words." (*ESV*, Romans 8:26). In order to be filled by the Holy Spirit, you first must have faith, as you receive Jesus Christ by faith. Second, you must surrender your life. Third, you must confess your sins.

**Faith:** We are filled by the Holy Spirit, by faith, in the same way that we received Jesus Christ by faith. It is by grace that we are saved through the blood of Jesus, not by our works. For it is by grace you have been saved, through faith—and this is not from yourselves, it is the gift of God—not by works, so that no one can boast. **(NIV, Ephesians 2:8,9)**

**Surrender:** We have to trust in God and let His will in our life be the way. Stop driving, and let God be in control of your life. Prepare to be totally willing to surrender your life to our Lord Jesus Christ. Prepare to convert from being self-serving to serving God. Let go of your sinful pleasures.

"Therefore I urge you, brethren, by the mercies of God, to present your bodies a living and holy sacrifice, acceptable to God, *which is* your spiritual service of worship. And do not be conformed to this world, but be transformed by the renewing of your mind, so that you may prove what the will of God is, that which is good and acceptable and perfect," **(Romans 12:1-9) (NASB,)**

**Confess:** Confess every sin that you know of, and experience the cleansing and forgiveness that God promises. "If we confess our sins, He is faithful and righteous to forgive us our sins and to cleanse us from all unrighteousness," **(ESV, 1John 1:19)**

When you receive Jesus Christ as your Lord and Savior, the Holy Spirit will dwell inside of you, even though you may not always feel its presence. The Holy Spirit is not given to you so that you might have a great emotional experience, but so that you might live a holy life and be a faithful witness for Christ. Remember, as Luke says, "how *much more* shall your heavenly Father give the Holy Spirit to them that ask him?" **(Luke 11:13)** So if you want to receive the Holy Spirit, ask Him now :

*Heavenly Father, I am a believer. I am Your child, and You are my Father. Jesus is my Lord. I believe with all my heart that Your Word is true. Your Word says if I will ask, I will receive the Holy Spirit. So in the name of Jesus Christ, my Lord, I am asking You to fill me to overflowing with Your precious Holy Spirit. In Jesus name Amen.*

So if you sinful people know how to give good gifts to your children,

How much more will your heavenly Father give the Holy Spirit

To those who ask him? **(NLT, Luke 11:13)**

*Ask, and it shall be given you; seek, and ye shall find; knock, and it shall be opened unto you: For every one that asketh receiveth; and he that seeketh findeth; and to him that knocketh it shall be opened.*

Matthew 7:7,8

©GOSPELGIFS

---

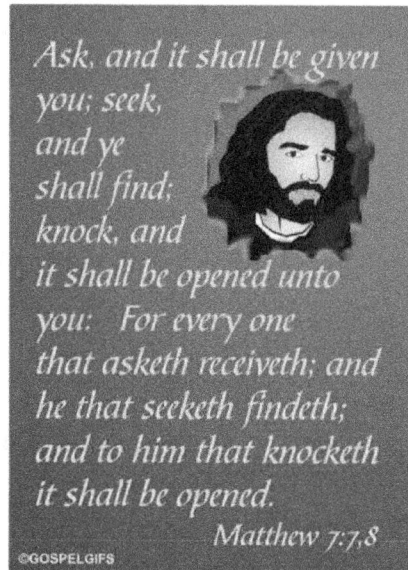

### The Holy Spirit

**Assignment:** Write down three to five challenges you would like the Holy Spirit to help you with then pray to God asking him to help you in these areas.

**Action:** Read the book of Acts to learn about the power of the Holy Spirit. Journal your thoughts.

1) _____

2) _____

3) _____

4) _____

5) _____

Journaling your thoughts and feelings helps you process events and release emotions. Journaling is a great tool for problem solving. Throughout this workbook you will find pages to journal your thoughts and dreams, and to document prayer requests and testimonials.

# JOURNAL

*Write down your thoughts and share them with the group.*

Date: _____

_____

_____

_____

_____

_____

_____

_____

_____

_____

_____

_____

_____

_____

_____

_____

_____

_____

_____

_____

_____

_____

> For God speaks again and again, though people do not recognize it. He speaks in dreams, in visions of the night, when deep sleep falls on people as they lie in their beds. He whispers in their ears and terrifies them with warnings. He makes them turn from doing wrong; he keeps them from pride. He protects them from the grave, from crossing over the river of death. **(Job 33:14-18) (NLT)**

# DREAM JOURNAL

Day: _____          Date: _____

Bedtime: _____          Time Awake: _____

**Dream Details:**

_____

_____

_____

_____

_____

_____

_____

**Significance or Symbolism:**

_____

_____

_____

_____

# 6. The Fruit Of The Spirit

The more we spend time learning about the Gospel of Jesus Christ and the word of God, the more fruits God will give us to help us become Christ-like. Fruits given to us by God include:

**Love**: Apostle Paul's description of "agape" love in 1 Corinthians, is about a sacrificial love, demonstrated by Jesus' death on the cross: "Love is patient, love is kind. It does not envy, it does not boast, it is not proud. It is not rude, it is not self-seeking, it is not easily angered, it keeps no record of wrongs. Love does not delight in evil but rejoices with the truth. It always protects, always trusts, always hopes, always perseveres. Love never fails," **(NIV, 1 Corinthians 13:4-8)**

**Joy**: Joy is a Spirit-given expression that flourishes best in hard times—meaning that a joyful person is happy inside even when external circumstances are not great. For example, the Thessalonians were under great stress due to persecution. And yet, in the midst of it all, they continued to experience great joy. Joy is not a human-based happiness that comes and goes; rather, true joy is divine in its origin. "The joy of the Lord is your strength" **(NLT, Nehemiah 8:10)**

**Peace**: Peace is not the absence of conflict, but the presence of God, no matter what the conflict. True peace comes from the Lord: "Therefore, since we have been justified through faith, we have peace with God through our Lord Jesus Christ," **(Romans 5:1 (NKJV)** "Peace I leave with you, My peace I give to you; not as the world gives to you. Let not your heart be troubled, neither let it be afraid,"
**(John 14:27) (NKJV)** "My people will live in peaceful dwelling places, in secure homes in undisturbed places of rest," **(NIV, Isaiah 32:18)**

**Long-suffering (patience):** "Patient" or "long-suffering" describes a person who may have the power to exercise revenge, but instead exercises restraint. When we pray about something that may take years to come to fruition, it takes patience to wait for the blessing of our prayers being answered. We are "strengthened with all might, according to his glorious power, unto all patience and long-suffering with joyfulness," **(KJV, Colossians 1:11)**

**Gentleness (kindness)**: Kindness means doing a good or selfless deed without expecting anything in return. Kindness means respecting and helping others without waiting for that help to be returned. This may be helping or showing kindness to a homeless person on the street. We should live "in purity, understanding, patience and kindness; in the Holy Spirit and in sincere love; in truthful speech and in the power of God; with weapons of righteousness in the right hand and in the left."
**(NIV, 2 Corinthians 6:6-7)**

**Goodness:** Goodness describes a life characterized by deeds motivated by righteousness and the desire to be a blessing. Goodness is a moral characteristic of a Spirit-filled person. God is good; by repenting to God we turn away from bad things and from dishonesty. "Wherefore also we pray always for you, that our God would count you worthy of this calling, and fulfill all the good pleasure of his goodness, and the work of faith with power," **(KJV, 2 Thessalonians 1:11)** "For the fruit of the Spirit is in all goodness and righteousness and truth." **(KJV, Ephesians 5:9)**

**Faith (faithfulness):** We must trust God, even when He is silent and when we see no miracles. Trust is part of faithfulness. We know God is reliable, steadfast, and true. Being faithful requires personal resolve not to wander away from our commitments and promises. Being a loyal Christian requires trust and faith in God. "I pray that out of His glorious riches He may strengthen you with power through His Spirit in your inner being, so that Christ may dwell in your hearts through faith." **(NIV, Ephesians 3:16-17)**

**Meekness:** Meekness or gentleness does not mean weakness. Rather, gentleness involves humility and thankfulness to God, as well as polite, restrained behavior toward others. The opposites of gentleness are anger, a desire for revenge, and self-aggrandizement. Gentleness can mean holding something delicately, as if it might break. We should treat not only objects but situations in a gentle manner, even when we are angry. Remain gentle in action. Stand up for yourself in a gentle way. "Brethren, if a man be overtaken in a fault, ye which are spiritual, restore such a one in the spirit of meekness; considering thyself, lest thou also be tempted," **(KJV, Galatians 6:1)** "With all lowliness and meekness, with long-suffering, forbearing one another in love," **(KJV, Ephesians 4:2)**

**Temperance (self-control):** Self-control is, obviously, the ability to control oneself and one's actions. We must have control over what we say and do in order for us to live as God would like for us to live. When we want to react to someone in anger in the heat of the moment, we must instead back down and resolve the situation calmly. As the saying goes, "let go and let God." Temperance involves moderation, constraint, and the ability to say "no" to our baser desires and fleshly lusts. "For this very reason, make every effort to add to your faith goodness; and to goodness, knowledge; and to knowledge, self-control; and to self-control, perseverance; and to perseverance, godliness; and to godliness, mutual affection; and to mutual affection, love," **(NIV, 2 Peter 1:5-7)**

## Assignment:

On a scale of 1 – 10, with 10 being your best, how would you currently rate yourself in each fruit of the spirit? The closer we become to God, the nearer Our numbers will be to a 10.

**Fruit of the Spirit: My Rating:** _____

1) "Love"              1  2  3  4  5  6  7  8  9  10

2) "Joy"               1  2  3  4  5  6  7  8  9  10

3) "Peace"             1  2  3  4  5  6  7  8  9  10

4) "Long-suffering"    1  2  3  4  5  6  7  8  9  10

5) "Gentleness"        1  2  3  4  5  6  7  8  9  10

6) "Goodness"          1  2  3  4  5  6  7  8  9  10

7) "Faith"             1  2  3  4  5  6  7  8  9  10

8) "Meekness"          1  2  3  4  5  6  7  8  9  10

9) "Temperance"        1  2  3  4  5  6  7  8  9  10

For the fruit of the Spirit is in all goodness and righteousness and truth; ~Eph 5:9

```
S U L E E C G G E S U S T
S O O E G O O F N T O U E
E C N A R E P M E T N S O
N G G S A F A I T H E H O
K S S G S C P O E L O N O
E U U O C E E E K O O O G
E T F O O P N R S S S V U
M P F D S E E E N O P N E
I E E N E T Y P L E N G S
O N R E O O E R I T S N G
E A I S J A G C G G N N S
M R N S C N T H E Y F E K
E T G E P E G E O N C T G
```

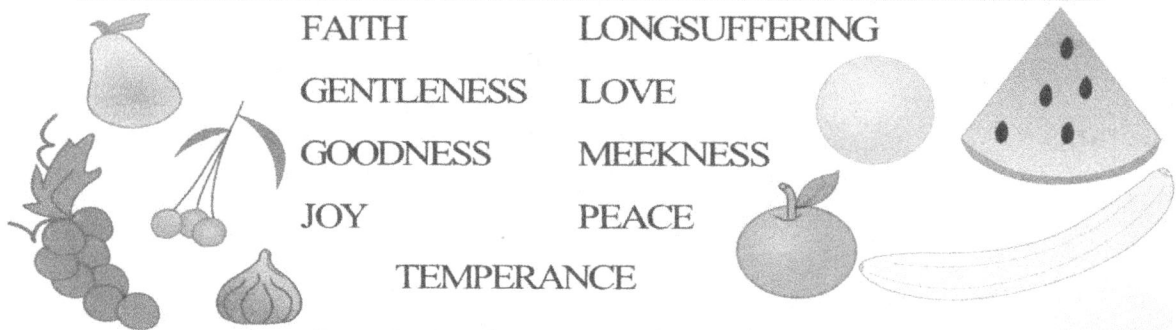

FAITH            LONGSUFFERING

GENTLENESS       LOVE

GOODNESS         MEEKNESS

JOY              PEACE

TEMPERANCE

Unscramble the words and write them in the corresponding blanks. Then take the letters in the circles and arrange them to find the solution to the puzzle.

EECAP      _ _ ◯ _ _

TAFIH      _ _ ◯ _ _

SLGEEENSNT _ _ _ _ _ _ _ _ ◯ _

DESONSGO   _ _ _ _ _ ◯ _ ◯ _

MEEPTNEARC ◯ _ ◯ _ _ _ _ _ _ _

EMESKNSE   _ _ _ ◯ _ _ ◯ _

EVOL       _ _ _ ◯

YJO        ◯ _ _

GIGUNFRNFESLO _ _ _ _ _ _ ◯ _ _ _ _ _

Fruit of the Spirit - How we get it.

_ _ _ _ _ _ _ _ _ _ _ _ _ _

Answers on page 193

But the fruit of the Spirit is love, joy, peace, long-suffering, gentleness,

Goodness, faith, meekness, temperance: against such there is no law.

**(KJV, Galatians 5:22-23)**

How can a guy be pure in a society so sick with sin?

By walking in step with what God says.

How can a young man keep his way pure? By paying attention to Your word.
Psalm 119:9

GospelGifs

---

### The Fruit Of The Spirit

**Action:** On each one of the fruits of the spirit ask these questions:
1. Is this Fruit working in me?
2. How do I now show this Fruit in my daily life?
3. What blocks this Fruit from working and being exhibited in me?

**Review your rates from 1-10 on the fruits of the spirit. You can see the areas that need attention.**

We cannot get The fruit of the Spirit by our own nature. They are led by the Holy Spirit (God). Obedience to God's word and turning away from sin will produce these spiritual fruits in us. We need to pray to God to help us make the changes in our lives to become more Christ like. And to ask God for the gifts of the spirit.

**Use your journal to write down your thoughts. Share your testimony of any changes in your new relationship with God.**

Journaling your thoughts and feelings helps you process events and release emotions. Journaling is a great tool for problem solving. Throughout this workbook you will find pages to journal your thoughts and dreams, and to document prayer requests and testimonials.

# JOURNAL

*Write down your thoughts and share them with the group.*

Date: _____

_____

_____

_____

_____

_____

_____

_____

_____

_____

_____

_____

_____

_____

_____

_____

_____

_____

_____

_____

_____

_____

For God speaks again and again, though people do not recognize it. He speaks in dreams, in visions of the night, when deep sleep falls on people as they lie in their beds. He whispers in their ears and terrifies them with warnings. He makes them turn from doing wrong; he keeps them from pride. He protects them from the grave, from crossing over the river of death. **(Job 33:14-18) (NLT)**

# DREAM JOURNAL

Day: _____          Date: _____

Bedtime: _____          Time Awake: _____

**Dream Details:**

_____

_____

_____

_____

_____

_____

_____

**Significance or Symbolism:**

_____

_____

_____

_____

_____

# 7. The Kingdom

For unto us a child is born, unto us a son is given: and the government shall be upon his shoulder: and his name shall be called Wonderful, counselor, The mighty God, The everlasting Father, The Prince of Peace. King James Version **(Isaiah 9:6 KJV)**

"The law and the prophets were until John. Since that time The kingdom of God has been preached, and everyone is pressing into it." **(Luke 16:16 NKJV)**

Now after John was put in prison, Jesus came to Galilee, preaching the gospel of the kingdom of God, [and] saying, "The time is fulfilled, and the kingdom of God is at hand. Repent, and believe in the gospel." **(Mark 1:14-18)**

The Kingdom of God is self sufficient and has everything that anyone would need. Jesus talks about the Kingdom and the power of the Kingdom that he is bringing. The Pharisees asked Jesus when will this Kingdom that you're talking about come. Jesus reply was, "The kingdom of God does not come with observation; [21] nor will they say, 'See here!' or 'See there! For indeed, the kingdom of God is within you." **( Luke 17:19-22 NKJV)** So Jesus is saying this Kingdom is not a Kingdom you will see with the eye, this Kingdom cannot be pointed out like when you're going shopping, looking for a store, and you say - oh there it is! This Kingdom is invisible. There will be a day ahead when the Kingdom of heaven will be a physical Kingdom. That day is when the city of God comes down out of heaven and will sit upon the earth, but right now it is in the midst. The Kingdom is within.

As believers we are in this powerful Kingdom that has everything we need, given to us when we receive Jesus as our Lord and Savior. Let's read the proof in the text, "Giving thanks to the Father, who has qualified us to share in the inheritance of the saints in Light. For He rescued us from the domain of darkness, and transferred us to the kingdom of His beloved Son, 14 in whom we have redemption, the forgiveness of sins." **( Colossians 1:12-20) (NASB)**

God has transferred us which means to move from one place to another, to take from one hand to another, so God has spiritually moved us to have full access to the inheritance of the Kingdom of light.

When you think of an inheritance it comes from a passing at the owner's death or a birthright. So now we have moved into this new Kingdom. This Kingdom functions by faith. We have our health care in this kingdom, our economy, strength, joy, peace, and blessings are in this kingdom.

We walk in the blessings of salvation and preach about the gospel of salvation but rarely do we speak about the Gospel of the Kingdom.

We are saved but are not getting the fullness of the Kingdom. We find ourselves oppressed; saved but sick. One reason is because we have moved into the Kingdom of light with a Kingdom of darkness mindset. Since we were kids we have been engraved with a wrong outlook on what a successful life is. We develop an image of what the world thinks. We mimic their customs and behavior. True success is knowing what your God given purpose in life is and having the wisdom to apply it.

Even though we are in the blessing of the Kingdom of light which has everything we need we still think like the world thinks, because our training comes from being born into the kingdom of darkness. We say things like, "I am broke." "I have no real purpose." This is because we have a mindset from a kingdom that operates in inferiority. We go by what our bank account may look like or how we feel rather than what God says. Now if the kingdom of light comes with no observation then we cannot always believe in what we see or feel because our kingdom operates on faith, and faith is the substance of things hoped for, the evidence of things not seen. **(Ephesians 4:31-32) (NIV)**

Now you can see we are observing two Kingdoms. God is showing us the kingdom of darkness and the Kingdom of light. There are two worlds in effect right now. One is superior and one is inferior. We have two systems in operation; one operates in fear and one operates in faith. We have a two-system lifestyle; the Kingdom of Heaven and the Kingdom of darkness (that has a Babylonian lifestyle). When God transferred us to the kingdom of His beloved Son nothing more than a change from us was required.

God warns us, "Don't copy the behavior and customs of this world, but let God transform you into a new person by changing the way you think. Then you will learn to know God's will for you, which is good and pleasing and perfect." **(Romans 12:2 NLT)** God said let me transform you into a new person. This is why we become born again, and Jesus told Nicodemus, a ruler of the Jews, "Truly, truly, I say to you, unless one is born again he cannot see the kingdom of God." Nicodemus said to him, "How can a man be born when he is old? Can he enter a second time into his mother's womb and be born?" Jesus answered, "Truly, truly, I say to you, unless one is born of water and the Spirit, he cannot enter the kingdom of God. [6] That which is born of the flesh is flesh, and that which is born of the Spirit is spirit.

Think about how our natural birth is of the flesh, but God said when we receive Jesus Christ as our Lord and Savior he will dwell within us. Remember when Jesus stood and cried out, saying, "[] If anyone is thirsty, let him come to Me and drink. He who believes in Me, as the Scripture said, 'From his innermost being will flow rivers of living water. This all makes total sense. The Kingdom of light is a total transformation. You're walking now in the spirit of God. The Holy Spirit is in you, teaching you the secrets of the kingdom. God said, "Let me transform you into a new person by changing the way you think. And Jesus said that we are not "of the world" just like he is not. **(John 17:14) (ESV)**

God has moved us to another place. This is why it is impossible to please God without faith, because the kingdom of light runs on faith in the unseen. God said let me transform you. He is saying to "just say yes." Believe and I will show you. Come follow me, and leave the cares of the world behind. We cannot see or hear God because we are looking through the lens of the kingdom of darkness. We are too busy as people, pleasing and thinking like the Rich man, a Ruler holding on to what is seen rather than the promises of God. This is one of the reasons why Jesus spoke in Parables.

# The Purpose of the Parables

[10] Then the disciples came and said to him, "Why do you speak to them in parables?" [11] And he answered them, "To you it has been given to know the secrets of the kingdom of heaven, but to them it has not been given. [12] For to the one who has, more will be given, and he will have an abundance, but from the one who has not, even what he has will be taken away. [13] This is why I speak to them in parables, because seeing they do not see, and hearing they do not hear, nor do they understand. **(Mathew 13:9-15)**

When we seek God and read His Word there will be some things we may not fully understand, but we keep approaching Him regardless, and He will then open our eyes and help us see. The little understanding that we get will lead to a greater understanding as we continue to search and study God's Word. A person who may think he has all he needs, who does not apply himself to trying to learn more, will lose ground in the amount that he understands. We have to seek God with the right motives. When Jesus asked the disciples to follow Him they left families and friends, and elected to learn the truth about the Kingdom. As believers we have to seek God and take our own personal journeys to build a relationship with Him. The more you spend time with God, the better He will release the secrets of the kingdom. We need not just the knowledge of the kingdom that Jesus brought, but the understanding.

When we see these two Kingdoms that are in operation - the kingdom of darkness and the kingdom of light – we also see that they act differently, speak differently, and respond differently. When you share about how you enjoy going to church and praising God for His mercy and grace, we give Him all the glory for the awesome things He is doing in our life. When we talk about the King God and his Kingdom you will see how some look at you strangely, as if you were talking about something fictitious. Their mindset is different. They do not speak or think the way we think. We have to keep our eyes on the Lord regardless of any backlash on our walk with God.

What I am saying, dear brothers and sisters, is that our physical bodies cannot inherit the Kingdom of God. These dying bodies cannot inherit what will last forever.

[51] But let me reveal to you a wonderful secret. We will not all die, but we will all be transformed! [52] It will happen in a moment, in the blink of an eye, when the last trumpet is blown. For when the trumpet sounds, those who have died will be raised to live forever. And we who are living will also be transformed. [53] For our dying bodies must be transformed into bodies that will never die; our mortal bodies must be transformed into immortal bodies. [54] Then, when our dying bodies have been transformed into bodies that will never die, [a] this Scripture will be fulfilled:"Death is swallowed up in victory. O death, where is your victory? O death, where is your sting?" **(1 Corinthians 15:50-55 New Living Translation) (NLT)**

71

# BEATITUDES OF JESUS
### (Sermon on the Mount)

## *Matthew 5:1-12*

## The beatitudes describe the character of the people of the Kingdom of God

### "Blessed are the poor in spirit, for theirs is the kingdom of heaven."

We must humble ourselves and look to God because we know all the blessings come from Him. We know that God is merciful and we cannot get into the Kingdom by anything that we have done, only by the grace of God. We know we need Jesus Christ to be saved. The strong in spirit can become prideful and do not recognize the need for God. Do not think of yourselves more highly than you ought. Be grateful for what you have been given.

### "Blessed are they who mourn, for they shall be comforted."

We feel shame, hurt and regret because of the sins we have committed against God. We feel sorrowful because of our sinful nature and the amount of sin is so great. However God's grace covers all who come to Him and repent and ask for mercy. The Holy Spirit will comfort us in our sorrow. We turn from our sins because we have a strong desire for God over sin. We mourn because of the disobedience.

### "Blessed are the meek, for they shall inherit the earth."

We never give in to offenses and pettiness, because we know vengeance is God's. We are able to turn the other cheek knowing that 'an eye for an eye' is in error. God repays and we put our trust in Him. We endure injury with patience and without resentment. We look for peace in all situations. A person who is meek will not be moved by insults. We know that anything good we accomplish is from God.

### "Blessed are they who hunger and thirst for righteousness, for they shall be satisfied."

Just like when you hunger for food, the desire to eat and fill your belly is the way you feel about the word of God. You hunger for His teachings and the secrets of the kingdom. To quench our thirst we speak and teach about the Gospel. We do not hunger and thirst for riches, honors, and pleasures of this world. We hunger for the refilling of the Holy Spirit and righteousness before God, the righteousness that comes from the forgiveness of sins. We do the things that please God, we hunger for spiritual food.

72

### "Blessed are the merciful, for they shall obtain mercy."

We show mercy to someone who has caused us injury or pain. We are imitating God and are also in obedience to his word. If we then show mercy to the poor, the wretched, the guilty, it shows that we are like God. We must give what God has given us - mercy. To show mercy is very delightful and desirable by God; it is what He requires. God has shown His mercy by giving His Son to die for us. We should look for the good qualities in people, and easily forgive. Do not hold grudges.

### "Blessed are the pure of heart, for they shall see God."

We desire change because we know God looks at the heart and not the outward appearance. We are concerned with our behavior because we know we are saved and filled with the Holy Spirit, and though we know we have a sinful nature, we press on, driving to do what is right even when we fall short. We get up, dust off and repent. It is not enough for us to correct our mistakes, we desire to have a Holy heart. We are careful of the things that we watch, read and hear. We fill our minds with good thoughts.

### "Blessed are the peacemakers, for they shall be called the children of God."

We strive for unity in the family and community, looking for any other way than war, fights, lawsuits, or death. It is being the middleman; the one who says it is really worth all this. We show the love of God by defusing the fire of anger and strife. Instead of fanning the fire of strife, we use our influence and wisdom to reconcile and adjust our differences, restoring them to a state of unity. We quickly speak up and do not allow division. We should work to keep the church in unity. It is wanting to be part of the solution toward unity and harmony among all people. We look for peace in all things.

### Blessed are they who are persecuted for the sake of righteousness, For theirs is the Kingdom of Heaven."

We speak the truth about the true living God, and some people will hate you for it. You speak about turning away from your sins because God wants a relationship with you, and often those you speak this too will mistreat you. They say how dare he or she, and they judge you harshly for following God's way. It is wanting to do what is right rather than what is wrong. We will often be treated unfairly because we live and breathe the Gospel of Jesus Christ, because we believe in Jesus Christ the Son of God.

**God warns his people in."(Proverbs 14:12 (NLT)** "There is a path before each person that seems right, but it ends in death.[50]

> **Romans 12:2 NLT** Don't copy the behavior and customs of this world, but let God transform you into a new person by changing the way you think. Then you will learn to know God's will for you, which is good and pleasing and perfect."

**Assignment:** God says not to copy the behavior and customs of this world. Circle the behaviors you would like to change and pray to God that He will help make these changes. Journal the consequences you had from these behaviors. Below are some examples of positive and negative behaviors.

| Positive | Negative |
|---|---|
| **Attitudes** | |
| Accepts authority | Rebellious |
| Forgiving | Unforgiving, holds grudges |
| Generosity | Greed, materialism |
| Caring | Uncaring, unfeeling |
| Rational-self control | Anger |
| Serve-help others | Want to be served |
| Faith | Faithless, cannot trust |
| Humble | Arrogant-conceited, prideful |
| Not jealous | Envy, jealousy |
| Selfless-self sacrificing | Selfish, self-serving |
| Love | Unloving, lust |
| Courageous | Cowering, fearful |
| Courteous | Rude, impolite |
| Peaceful | Chaos, eye for an eye |
| Freedom | Controlling |
| Goodwill | Malice, hatred |
| Hard-working | Lazy, sloth |
| Respectful | Disrespectful, rude |
| Self-confident | Lacks self confidence |
| Trusting | Suspicious, mistrusting |
| Giver- How can I help | Taker- looking out for self |
| Patient | Impatient |
| Grateful | Ungrateful |

Journaling your thoughts and feelings helps you process events and release emotions. Journaling is a great tool for problem solving. Throughout this workbook you will find pages to journal your thoughts and dreams, and to document prayer requests and testimonials.

# JOURNAL

*WRITE DOWN YOUR THOUGHTS AND SHARE WITH YOUR GROUP*

Date: _____

_____

_____

_____

_____

_____

_____

_____

_____

_____

_____

_____

_____

_____

_____

_____

_____

_____

_____

_____

_____

For God speaks again and again, though people do not recognize it. He speaks in dreams, in visions of the night, when deep sleep falls on people as they lie in their beds. He whispers in their ears and terrifies them with warnings. He makes them turn from doing wrong; he keeps them from pride. He protects them from the grave, from crossing over the river of death. **(Job 33:14-18) (NLT)**

# DREAM JOURNAL

Day: _____          Date: _____

Bedtime: _____          Time Awake: _____

**Dream Details:**

_____

_____

_____

_____

_____

_____

_____

**Significance or Symbolism:**

_____

_____

_____

_____

_____

# 8 The Power Of Prayer

God does not want us to pray for the applause of men. Don't pray to impress people with these long prayers. Prayer is about thanking and honoring God for who He is and showing gratitude for what He has done. God does not like us to babble and be so repetitious in our prayer. He is not looking for you to pray with many words. He knows all our needs even before we ask. It is better to have a heart with no words than words without a heart. We should approach God with the proper perspective.

I see new believers afraid to lead a prayer because they have learned through observation how many Christians pray very long drawn out prayers. This often makes a new believer feel inadequate to pray in front of a group, even though they have something worthwhile to contribute. Never feel that what is on your heart to pray about is inferior to what lengthy prayers have to say. God loves that you would speak up and honor Him with your humble heartfelt words, showing faith in the power of prayer and courage to be a prayer warrior. God shows us how he does not want us to pray in **(Mathew 6:5)**

"And when you pray, you must not be like the hypocrites. For they love to stand and pray in the synagogues and at the street corners, that they may be seen by others. Truly, I say to you, they have received their reward."

"And when you are praying, do not use meaningless repetition as the Gentiles do, for they suppose that they will be heard for their many words. [8] So do not be like them; for your Father knows what you need before you ask Him."

**Pray, then, in this way:**

Our Father which art in heaven, Hallowed be thy name. Thy kingdom come, Thy will be done in earth, as it is in heaven. Give us this day our daily bread. And forgive us our debts, as we forgive our debtors. And lead us not into temptation, but deliver us from evil: For thine is the kingdom, and the power, and the glory, forever. Amen. **(Matthew 6:9-15) (KJV)**

And My people who are called by My name humble themselves and pray and seek My face and turn from their wicked ways, then I will hear from heaven, and will forgive their sin and will heal their land. **(2 Chronicles 7:14 NASB)**

## Jesus Cleanses the Temple

Now the Passover of the Jews was at hand, and Jesus went up to Jerusalem. [14] And He found in the temple those who sold oxen and sheep and doves, and the moneychangers doing business. [15] When He had made a whip of cords, He drove them all out of the temple, with the sheep and the oxen, and poured out the changers' money and overturned the tables. [16] And He said to those who sold doves, "Take these things away! Do not make My Father's house a house of merchandise!" [17] Then His disciples remembered that it was written, "Zeal for Your house has eaten Me up." John 2:13-25 (New King James Version)

Prayer is so powerful. Jesus was showing his anger. He wanted the people to know nothing will come without God first. God has to be honored and respected in His Holy places. You do not see Jesus get so angry until people disrespect a place of worship. As Christians we must have this same type of passion for God in all things. We cannot serve two Gods!

The disciples saw so many miracles done by Jesus, yet the only thing they asked of Jesus was to teach them how to pray. They did not ask God to teach them to walk on water, only how to pray. Prayer is a personal relationship with God. Jesus went away to be alone with the Father. The disciples saw Him go off alone and pray. They knew the power in prayer. The Interaction Jesus had with God was through prayer. The powerful things Jesus was able to do was through the Father. Jesus would get up in the early mornings to pray. The disciples saw Jesus do this and then He would go out and heal people and raise people from the dead. Jesus was a problem solver!

Today people spend a few minutes a day with God and find themselves suffering with the same problems for years. Before we do anything God wants us to spend time with Him first. Time in prayer is the best investment you can make. Take some time in your day to thank God for all the great things He has done for you and your family. You can start off just a few minutes a day in prayer and slowly build a relationship with God. Soon you will find yourself talking about God, saying how great God is and thanking Him in the car or on a bike ride. Putting Him first in your daily situations will cause you to see the power of God in all things. God need's us to impact our communities. Just like he used Moses to help get the people out of Egypt. He used Abraham and Noah for His purpose too. God gave us the dominion over the earth and needs us to work with Him. God cannot use us if we cannot hear Him. We must know what God sounds like. We have to spend time in prayer and follow his commands. The more we are God-conscious the more we can know when God is talking to us, and the better we will understand what He is saying. Prayer is not an option; it is a must.

Pray to God for healing, not to feel good. God is not looking for us to only feel good. God knows when we are healthy. God can use us for His sake. So pray for healing in your mind, body, and soul. An important part of prayer time is when we listen, and also when we are silent so that God can hear what is in your heart without you always needing words to say it.

# Starting a prayer Journal

NEVER STOP PRAYING    ALWAYS BELIEVE

On the first page of the Prayer journal, I start listing requests. I start with my constant prayers. My relationship with Christ, my relationship with my family, the salvation of my friends and family… instead of writing the date beside these requests, I write the word **Constant**.

After I list the constant prayers on my heart, I start in with those who are sick as well as other needs of my friends and family. If there are requests from last year that have not been answered yet, I keep them in my constant prayer list.

When there is an answer to a prayer request, I will write in the praise report space how the Lord answered that prayer. For example, last year we had been praying for a friend to get a job and she finally got a job working for the state, so beside her name in the praise report, I wrote: "God blessed her with a job" and then the date.

**P**raise God

**R**epent

**A**sk God to intervene in your life

**Y**ield to God and follow his commands.

# Prayer Journal

**Starting a prayer Journal will help you stay in prayer for you, your friends, and your family.**

| DATE | PRAYER REQUEST | PRAISE REPORT |
|---|---|---|
| **Constant** | My family | |
| **Constant** | Salvation of my friends and family | |
| **Constant** | My relationship with God | |
| | | |
| | | |
| | | |
| | | |
| | | |
| | | |
| | | |
| | | |
| | | |
| | | |
| | | |
| | | |
| | | |
| | | |
| | | |
| | | |
| | | |
| | | |
| | | |
| | | |
| | | |

# Prayer Journal

**Starting a prayer Journal will help you stay in prayer for you, your friends, and your family.**

| DATE | PRAYER REQUEST | PRAISE REPORT |
|------|----------------|---------------|
|      |                |               |
|      |                |               |
|      |                |               |
|      |                |               |
|      |                |               |
|      |                |               |
|      |                |               |
|      |                |               |
|      |                |               |
|      |                |               |
|      |                |               |
|      |                |               |
|      |                |               |
|      |                |               |
|      |                |               |
|      |                |               |
|      |                |               |
|      |                |               |
|      |                |               |
|      |                |               |
|      |                |               |
|      |                |               |

# Prayer Journal

Starting a prayer Journal will help you stay in prayer for you, your friends, and your family.

| DATE | PRAYER REQUEST | PRAISE REPORT |
| --- | --- | --- |
| | | |
| | | |
| | | |
| | | |
| | | |
| | | |
| | | |
| | | |
| | | |
| | | |
| | | |
| | | |
| | | |
| | | |
| | | |
| | | |
| | | |
| | | |
| | | |
| | | |
| | | |
| | | |
| | | |
| | | |
| | | |

# A Turn In My Belly
## (My Testimony)

I remember it was 2002 and I was doing really well in Sacramento, California. I had just moved from San Francisco and not long after I had built a thriving business. I bought my first home while my business continued to grow, and I did not want for anything at that time. I remember I was at work one day and suddenly felt like something was missing. This was the first time I understood what people meant when they said they had been called to seek God.

Even though everything at this time was going well for me, there was a tug at my heart. Despite my prosperity I felt empty. I started thinking about God. I was so ignorant about who God was, or why I was even looking for Him. I started going to church. None of my friends attended church. I was on a mission looking for what was missing in my life, and what was missing was God! I began to learn about how He gave his son Jesus for our sins. I had heard about God and Jesus because I was raised as a Catholic when very young, but I grew up without a relationship with God. So here I am a divorced woman in her 30's alone on my Journey looking for Him.

Everything was going well and I loved the church I started to attend, but as time went on I noticed every time I turned around the church wanted money outside of the tithe and offering, and we never served and I had a hunger to serve. I started to go to fellowship outside of regular church service at one of the group leaders' houses, and she would also ask for an offering for the pastor during fellowship time. I started feeling uncomfortable as I would look around the room and say to myself, "Why am I even here? We are all saved. We know Jesus. We should be out feeding the hungry or serving in some kind of capacity." Yes we were all blessed, but my heart was hungry for helping people in need!

Every morning I would get up about 2am and pray, asking God if I could be a part of His team. I did not know what all that entailed. I just felt in my heart that Jesus is the only way, and serving was my calling. I loved Jesus and I cherished every word the pastor spoke about Jesus. I loved that He died for me. That in itself made me in awe of Him. I wanted to know more about Jesus. I also began thinking differently once I found out the truth about Jesus. God showed me the power He gave the believer, the power to be used for change in our family and in our communities. I would think –Wow! All this time I was living without the true knowledge of Jesus! I knew there was a God, but I was missing the Son and the Holy Spirit. I know God was aware that I always loved Him. I was just ignorant to His Word and commands because I had been misguided, but God's Word says, "My sheep hear My voice, and I know them, and they follow Me." **(John 10:27 NKJV)**

No matter how much of a sinner I was, God knew I believed in Him. God called me. I know He did. I would always read the book of Acts. I was so drawn to how powerful God truly is and the gifts that were available to us. Gifts like speaking in the Spirit. Gifts like interpreting dreams and prophecy or seeing visions. I wanted to speak to God, and only He would understand what I was saying. When we do not know what to pray for, the Spirit *will* know what to pray for - all the awesome things the Holy Spirit can help you with! I wanted all the gifts He said he would give. I would read the bible and all kinds of books on hearing from God. I would go to retreats. I was really seeking Him!

I remember that Sunday morning I went to church and the pastor started talking about how they needed some money for the floors in the day care. Someone started an auction by saying, "Can I get $1,000 over here? Okay, how about over there?" I was so embarrassed. I felt like, wow! We are supposed to be having a church service and instead we are doing an auction! I felt like I could not afford to go to church. How wrong is this type of thinking? When I got home I was really turned off from church. I remember saying how I was not going back. On the inside I was thinking, don't give up on God! I loved giving tithes and offerings, but everything was money-focused and we never served.

That afternoon I went into my living room and got on my knees and said, "God, the only reason why I went to church was to learn more about you. I wanted to hear the word of God, but I am not going back because I do not feel that they are helping anyone but themselves." I remember right before I left my living room I felt moved to pray the Our Father prayer. So I got down on my knees and as I began to recite the Our Father prayer, an imaginary doorknob in the middle of my belly turned. It was as if I felt a release, as if my belly had an actual doorknob and someone turned and opened it! And then, as I started praying the Our Father prayer, I started speaking in another language (Tongues) and these spiritual words just were flowing out! I was shocked by the feeling and amazed by the language, and how it sounds. To this day I will never ever forget the feeling of that turn in my belly. It was evidence of the Holy Spirit releasing one of the gifts that I asked God for.

God will give you the gifts of the Holy Spirit! Just seek God diligently, and ask Him! The good news is a few weeks later a friend had invited me to her church. I went and as we worshiped I looked around and saw all ages, all nationalities, and the love of God in the Pastor. Since that day I have never left this church. I have been attending services there for over 7 years now. I joined hospitality at the church and got involved in feeding the homeless, and in serving my community. I started getting connected with people who loved to serve like I did.

Not long after I joined the Aglow Prison Ministry. We minister to women who are incarcerated. We believe in telling the good news of Jesus Christ, to bring life and hope through faith in Him and to minister through prayer and fellowship, praise and worship, showing and teaching unconditional love through Jesus Christ our Lord and Savior.

Since I have gotten closer to God, I have made major changes in my life. I stopped using drugs and drinking alcohol. I gave my business to a friend and went back to school, and I am now a Caadac Certified Alcohol and drug counselor. Since I started seeking God, I have grown so much, and I have found an inner peace. I have learned God has a plan for us, and as long as we do not give up on God and come to Him in spirit and in truth, He will put us where we need to be. As we grow spiritually, He will use us in a mighty way for the Kingdom here on earth!

PUT ON THE WHOLE
ARMOR OF GOD

©GOSPELGIFS

# The Whole Armor of God

A final word: Be strong in the Lord and in His mighty power. Put on all of God's armor so that you will be able to stand firm against all strategies of the devil. For we are not fighting against flesh-and-blood enemies, but against evil rulers and authorities of the unseen world, against mighty powers in this dark world, and against evil spirits in the heavenly places.

Therefore, put on every piece of God's armor so you will be able to resist the enemy in the time of evil. Then after the battle you will still be standing firm. Stand your ground, putting on the belt of truth and the body armor of God's righteousness. For shoes, put on the peace that comes from the Good News so that you will be fully prepared. In addition to all of these, hold up the shield of faith to stop the fiery arrows of the devil. Put on salvation as your helmet, and take the sword of the Spirit, which is the word of God.

Pray in the Spirit at all times and on every occasion. Stay alert and be persistent in your prayers for all believers everywhere. **(Ephesians 6:10-20) (NLT)**

Every piece of the Armor of God has a purpose and every piece is for our protection. Now if God is telling us to put on all His armor it is because we cannot do anything with self. We need God and only He can fight our battles through us so we need to participate by faith and every day we need to put on the belt of truth. We never know when the season changes. One day everything is great, life is good, and then you find out you or someone has cancer, or a family member has been arrested. We cannot lose faith. Remember that everything God has spoken in his Word we can take to the bank, because God is not a father who would lie.

God said put on all of God's armor so that you will be able to stand firm against all strategies of the devil. When we look at the text it says God's armor. God has given us everything we need to be successful because we are not fighting against flesh-and-blood enemies, but against evil rulers and authorities of the unseen world, against mighty powers in this dark world, and against evil spirits in the heavenly places. Our battles are spiritual and unseen.

A perfect example of putting on the Armor of God is when Satan tried to deceive Jesus. Satan asked Jesus to worship him. Jesus shows you how to use the sword of the Spirit, which is the Word of God. Jesus told Satan, "Get away, Satan! It is written: 'The Lord, your God, shall you worship and Him alone shall you serve. After he stood on the Word, the devil left Him and, behold, angels came and ministered to Jesus. **(KJV, Matthew 4)**

God will always bring comfort to his children who are in battle while they stand on the Word of God. God will never leave us if we keep our faith in Him and do what He tells us to do. We must put on His armor to be successful in this wicked world.

# The Enemy The Devil

For we are not fighting against flesh-and-blood enemies, but against evil rulers and authorities of the unseen world, against mighty powers in this dark world, and against evil spirits in the heavenly places. Our enemy is Satan the devil and God has made it clear that we cannot win any battle against the devil and evil spirits unless we put on every piece of God's armor, so that you will be able to resist the enemy in the time of evil. Then after the battle you will still be standing firm. How can you be successful in any battle if you do not know about your opponent (Enemy) let alone how to use your armor (Weapons)?

So let's talk about our Enemy, who is Satan the devil, and his demon's. God said, "The thief's purpose is to steal, and kill, and destroy." "God's purpose is to give us a rich and satisfying life." God calls Satan a thief and tells us the only plan Satan has is to kill you, to steal from you, and to destroy you. This is written in **(John 10:10) (NLT)** I love the illustration Jesus gives.

### Jesus Illustration

[6] Those who heard Jesus that use this illustration didn't understand what he meant, [7] so he explained it to them: "I tell you the truth, I am the gate for the sheep. [8] All who came before me were thieves and robbers. But the true sheep did not listen to them. [9] Yes, I am the gate. Those who come in through me will be saved. They will come and go freely and will find good pastures. [10] The thief's purpose is to steal and kill and destroy. My purpose is to give them a rich and satisfying life.

[11] "I am the good shepherd. The good shepherd sacrifices his life for the sheep. [12] A hired hand will run when he sees a wolf coming. He will abandon the sheep because they don't belong to him and he isn't their shepherd. And so the wolf attacks them and scatters the flock. [13] The hired hand runs away because he's working only for the money and doesn't really care about the sheep.

[14] "I am the good shepherd; I know my own sheep, and they know me, [15] just as my Father knows me and I know the Father. So I sacrifice my life for the sheep. **( John 10:6-15 NLT)**

I love the way our Lord and Savior Jesus Christ shows the way that men of this world will not only mislead us but also abandoned us. We have to keep our faith in God and stand on what is written as Jesus did with Satan. Satan will steal the word of God by twisting God's words, as he did in the beginning.

When the serpent (Devil) came to talk Eve into disobeying God's command about eating from the 'tree of knowledge of good and evil,' he did it by raising a question. The devil said to Eve "You will surely not die. [5] For God knows that in the day you eat of it your eyes will be opened, and you will be like God, knowing good and evil."

Now once Eve ate of the fruit and shared some with Adam, and God found out, read what God said: [22] Then the LORD God said, "Behold, the man has become like one of Us, to know good and evil. And now, lest he put out his hand and take also of the tree of life, and eat, and live forever"— [23] therefore the LORD God sent him out of the garden of Eden to till the ground from which he was taken. [24] So He drove out the man; and He placed cherubim at the east of the Garden of Eden, and a flaming sword which turned every way, to guard the way to the tree of life. **(Genesis 3:4) ( KJV) (Genesis 3:22) (KJV)**

So we see how the devil can put lies in our head by raising questions and using deception. The devil knows when we go against God, our sin separates us from God, and without the armor of God we are defeated. If we continue to follow the devil and be disobedient to God's word it will only lead us to death, and this is the plan that the devil has. Everything God does Satan wants to pervert it, and bring confusion. The devil knows that time is everything and he is doing everything in his power to waste all of our time seeking things of the world rather than seeking God. We cannot waste any more time

God says, "The time is surely coming," says the Sovereign LORD, "when I will send a famine on the land -- not a famine of bread or water but of hearing the words of the LORD. 12 People will stagger everywhere from sea to sea, searching for the word of the LORD, running here and going there, but they will not find it. 13 Beautiful girls and fine young men will grow faint and weary, thirsting for the LORD's word. 14 And those who worship and swear by the idols of Samaria, Dan, and Beersheba will fall down, never to rise again." **(Amos 8:11-14) (NLT)**

The devil knows God and the mighty power of God. We cannot waste time. We have to put on the "Belt of truth" (The word of God). We have to know the word so we will know the truth about God's Kingdom and everything that comes with it. The *government* of God has world peace, happiness, health and all the promises that God gives the believer. To those who believe in the finished work of Jesus Christ our Lord and Savior, and only the ones who cry out to the Lord will be saved. Satan has been defeated and his time is running short, in the meantime we need to put on the armor of God.

### God's warning to all Christians:

"Stay alert! Watch out for your great enemy, the devil. He prowls around like a roaring lion, looking for someone to devour. [9] Stand firm against him, and be strong in your faith. Remember that your Christian brothers and sisters all over the world are going through the same kind of suffering.
**(1 Peter 5:8-9 (New Living Translation)**

God confirms that the devil is real and he is our enemy. A lot of people do not believe there is a devil and take God for granted, and find themselves defeated over and over again. God said to be strong in your faith by wearing the shield of faith, not only hearing The Word but applying it to your struggles and if you do, God says you will be victorious.

### Why did The Devil turn against God?

God created the devil but he was not always the enemy. The devil was a Cherub angel, which covered the throne of God. Angels would worship God. The devil walked where God ruled. We believe the devil was also a part of the worship music along with the other Angels. Some believe it because of the text in **Ezekiel 28:13-15:**

[13] Thou hast been in Eden the garden of God; every precious stone was thy covering, the sardius, topaz, and the diamond, the beryl, the onyx, and the jasper, the sapphire, the emerald, and the carbuncle, and gold: the workmanship of thy tabrets and of thy pipes was prepared in thee in the day that thou wast created.

And the verses in **Revelation 15:2:**

And I saw as it were a sea of glass mingled with fire: and them that had gotten the victory over the beast, and over his image, and over his mark, and over the number of his name, stand on the sea of glass, having the harps of God.

God described the devil as the most beautiful Angel. He was so beautiful! Just think of walking into the finest jewelry store and seeing the best of the best Gems, the sparkles, the colors that radiate when we look at these gorgeous gems. Some of us today still look for these beautiful stones. According to scripture the devil was covered in the finest ones. Let's look at the text in **(Ezekiel 28:13 NLT)**:

"You were in Eden, the garden of God. Your clothing was adorned with every precious stone--red carnelian, pale-green peridot, white moonstone, blue-green beryl, onyx, green jasper, blue lapis Lazuli, turquoise, and emerald--all beautifully crafted for you and set in the finest gold. They were given to you on the day you were created."

God described how He had given the devil the best, only the finest. He had everything. So what happened? According to scripture because of the beauty and power the devil had, he was anointed as a guardian cherub. For God ordained him. On the holy mount of God the devil walked among the fiery stones. The love, power, and beauty made him feel that he could be God. Just imagine how the other Angels looked up to the devil. He was a model of success and greatness. He walked with God and God ordained him. What could be better than that?

**(Ezekiel 28:14):** I ordained and anointed you as the mighty angelic guardian. You had access to the holy mountain of God and walked among the stones of fire.

God said that the devil was blameless in all he did from the day he was created until the day evil was found in him. **(Ezekiel 28:15)**

The devil turned against God. God seemed surprised until evil was found. How did the evil get there? God says it clearly in the text: **(Ezekiel 28:17)**

"Your heart was filled with pride because of all your beauty. Your wisdom was corrupted by your love of splendor. So I threw you to the ground and exposed you to the curious gaze of kings."

The devil forgot about his creator and what God had given him, and why. He was ungrateful. The devil let his beauty, power and position go to his head. If you look up the word splendor it means brilliant or gorgeous appearance. God said his beauty and brilliance corrupted his wisdom. The devil had gotten full of himself! God started to see the change in this beautiful creation, because God knows our heart -including the devils. This scripture tells us what Satan the devil was thinking, and how God read his heart in **Isaiah 14:12:**

## The devil's thoughts, ideas and plan:

" For thou hast said in thine heart, I will ascend into heaven, I will exalt my throne above the stars of God. I will sit also upon the mount of the congregation, in the sides of the north:

[14] I will ascend above the heights of the clouds; **I will be like the most High**.

    Satan (the devil) wanted to overthrow God. He wanted to be like the most high. He wanted to be a god. Being a beautiful anointed mighty angelic guardian was not good enough. Oh no! He wanted to be worshiped! The devil wanted to be praised at the highest level because he had become prideful and arrogant, self-centered and most of all - envious and jealous of God. Being with God was not good enough. Through free will and his extreme brightness, the devil developed plans and ideas to become a god. He abused the special power given to him by God, corrupting it. This caused him to fall out of heaven. **Isaiah 14:12 (KJV)**

    **Revelation 12:7-9 (KJV)**

[7] And there was war in heaven: Michael and his angels fought against the dragon; and the dragon fought and his angels, [8] And prevailed not; neither was their place found any more in heaven.

[9] And the great dragon was cast out, that old serpent, called <u>the</u> **Devil, and Satan,** which deceiveth the whole world: he was cast out into the earth, and his angels were cast out with him.

    Satan the devil is now apart from God. He chose to be divided and what is divided cannot stand. He wanted division in the Kingdom of God. He tries to make us fall by causing disobedient, prideful and arrogant behavior to come forward in us. If we let the devil mess with our mind, we also will become divided from God and feel like we can be God, and not need our creator. Without God in our lives, we begin to rely on our own understanding of things. We stay in a carnal mindset and start to believe that *we* are all we need, which causes us to become empty and lost. We reach for outer worldly things to comfort us, and these worldly desires cause us to grow distant from that small still voice within. We start to depend on the world to provide rather than God, and who is the God of this world? The devil!

    The devil wants from us what we would give God; our obedience, praise, worship, and most of all the devil wants our disbelief in God's plans to prosper you and not harm you - plans to give you hope and a future. The devil wants you to think God's promises were a failed attempt and the way the devil will do it is by deception, by **casting doubt in God's Word.** The devil will cause you to lose faith in God and start to live an ungodly life. This is found in the text Acts 13:10 "And said, Oh full of all subtlety and all mischief, *thou* child of the devil, ***thou* enemy of all righteousness**, wilt thou not cease to pervert the right ways of the Lord?"

    So if we are blinded by the enemy we will become mischievous, causing harm and doing evil, thus becoming corrupt, un-righteous and disobedient. If we decide to live an ungodly life through our choices and free will, we are in agreement with Satan the devil, and are trusting in the God of this world, unable to see or hear the Good News of Jesus Christ, because our armor of God is down and we have become unprotected.

Those who believe in Jesus Christ are protected because the Holy Spirit comes to live inside of us. This is a promised gift to the believer. The God of the world (the devil) is powerless against God Almighty when you are filled with the Holy Spirit. It is the spirit of God in the believer who helps you seek to live a righteous life. God fights for the believer. In this text it is written for our confirmation **1 John 4:4:KJV**

"Ye are of God, little children, and have overcome them because greater is **he that is in you**, than he that is in the world"

So it is God who dwells in the believer who overcomes, but the devil wants to devour the truth so he can use the unbeliever for his benefit, which will result in a physical and or spiritual death. It is written in the text **2 Corinthians 4:4 (NLT):**

"Satan, who is the god of this world, has blinded the minds of those who don't believe. They are unable to see the glorious light of the Good News. They don't understand this message about the glory of Christ, who is the exact likeness of God"

If Satan the devil can devour our faith in God he can usurp and use you for his purpose and you will become lost and confused which is not God's will.

**Definition of usurp**: To seize and hold (the power or rights of another, for example) by force or without legal authority. To take over or occupy without right. To take the place of (another) without legal authority.

Satan the devil can do this with **"deception."**

Satan the devil is too powerful for us to ever think we can overcome him without God our Father in us. It is self destructive to think we do not need God in our life. God tells us we need the full Armor of God. One thing Christians forget is that the devil can trick us through his many disguises. The devil is able to look to us as an Angel of light, so how can we discern when Satan the devil has usurped a person by speaking through them or pushing them into making wrong decisions with his temptations and **"deception"**?

## Satan disguises himself as an angel of light.

[14] But I am not surprised! Even Satan disguises himself as an angel of light. [15] So it is no wonder that his servants also disguise themselves as servants of righteousness. In the end they will get the punishment their wicked deeds deserve. **2 Corinthians 11:14-15 (NLT)**

Satan the devil will attack you by getting in your head and pointing out all the horrible things you have done. He attacks God's people day and night. He wants us to feel worthless by believing that our sins are greater than God. Turning away from sin will not be the only struggle we face. The memories of what we have done, and all the shame and guilt behind those memories are the devil's delight! He wants to get inside of our head and make us believe God could not or cannot forgive us, because our sin is so great. We become stagnate and cannot do the things that God has created us to do. Satan does this by making the sinner feel less than worthy and un-loved by God, because of our life choices that are displeasing to God. We have to put on the "**The Sword of the Spirit**" (God's Word) and know that we are not expected to be perfect. Repentance is a decision to cease sinning and begin serving God instead.

There can be no repentance unless there was a sin. Forgiveness is a process for change, and we have all fallen short of sinlessness. It is the love of Jesus Christ, who died for us sinners, that makes us worthy and sinless before God. Anyone who cry's out to the Lord is saved. Put all that guilt and shame that the devil reminds you of behind you. Say, "Satan get ye behind me because it is written that:"

"There is no condemnation for those who belong to Christ Jesus. [2] And because you belong to him, the power of the life-giving Spirit has freed you from the power of sin that leads to death. [3] The law of Moses was unable to save us because of the weakness of our sinful nature. So God did what the law could not do. He sent his own Son in a body like the bodies we sinners have. And in that body God declared an end to sin's control over us by giving his Son as a sacrifice for our sins." AMEN!! **(Romans: 8) (NLT)**

# Satan's Plan

### (Read it, even if you're busy, especially if you're too busy)

Satan called a worldwide convention of demons. In his opening address he said, "We can't keep Christians from going to church. We can't keep them from reading their Bibles and knowing the truth. We can't even keep them from forming an intimate relationship with their Savior. Once they gain that connection with Jesus, our power over them is broken. So let them go to their churches; let them have their covered dish dinners, but steal their time, so they don't have time to develop a real relationship with Jesus Christ. This is what I want you to do," said the devil. "Distract them from gaining hold of their Savior and maintaining that vital connection throughout their day!" "How shall we do this?" his demons shouted. "Keep them busy in the nonessentials of life and invent innumerable schemes to occupy their minds," he answered:

a.. Tempt them to spend, spend, spend, and borrow, borrow, borrow.

b.. Persuade the wives to go to work for long hours and the husbands to work 6-7 days each week, 10-12 hours a day, so they can afford their empty lifestyles.

c.. Keep them from spending time with their children. As their families fragment, soon, their homes will offer no escape from the pressures of work!

d.. Over-stimulate their minds by sending and reading text messages so that they cannot hear that 'still, small voice.'

e.. Entice them to play the radio or CD player whenever they drive...to keep the TV, VCR, and their PCs going constantly in their home and see to it that every store and restaurant in the world plays non-biblical music constantly. This will jam their minds and break that union with Christ.

f.. Fill the coffee tables with magazines and newspapers. Pound their minds with the news 24 hours a day. Invade their driving moments with billboards. Flood their mailboxes with junk mail, mail order catalogs, sweepstakes, and every kind of newsletter and promotional offering free products, services and false hopes.

g.. Keep skinny, beautiful models on the magazines and TV so their husbands will believe that outward beauty is what's important, and they'll become dissatisfied with their wives.

h.. Keep the wives too tired to love their husbands at night. Give them headaches too! If they don't give their husbands the love they need, they will begin to look elsewhere. That will fragment their families quickly!

I.. Give them Santa Claus to distract them from teaching their children the real meaning of Christmas.

j.. Give them an Easter bunny so they won't talk about his resurrection and power over sin and death.

k.. Even in their recreation, let them be excessive...have them return from their recreation exhausted. Keep them too busy to go out in nature and reflect on God's creation. Send them to amusement parks, sporting events, plays, concerts, and movies instead.

l.. Keep them busy, busy, busy! And when they meet for spiritual fellowship, they will leave with troubled consciences.

m.. For those who resist all the temptations of television and worldly pursuits, crowd their lives with so many good causes that they have no time to seek power from Jesus. Soon they will be working in their own strength, sacrificing their health and family for the good of the cause.

"It will work! It will work!!"

It was quite a plan! The demons went eagerly to their assignments causing Christians everywhere to have little time for their God or their families, and to have little or no time to tell others about the power of Jesus to change lives. I guess the question is, has the devil been successful at his scheme? You be the judge! Does "busy" mean:

B-eing
U-nder
S-atan's
Y-oke

(Author unknown)

As we build our relationship with God we have to make sure that we put God first in all we do and not to put anything before God it is what God requires from us:

**Master, which is the great commandment in the law?** [37] Jesus said unto him, Thou shalt love the Lord thy God with all thy heart, and with all thy soul, and with all thy mind. [38] This is the first and great commandment. [39] And the second is like unto it, Thou shalt love thy neighbor as thyself. [40] On these two commandments hang all the law and the prophets. **Matthew 22:36-40 (KJV)**

What we love the most and the things that we desire is where our heart will be. We must examine ourselves and do a day-to-day inventory in order to know the answer to this question, "Is God seated first in my life?" God is eternal, whereas Satan the devil is temporal and his days are numbered:

### The Fate Of The Enemy The Devil

[10] Then the devil, who had deceived them, was thrown into the fiery lake of burning sulfur, joining the beast and the false prophet. There they will be tormented day and night forever and ever. **Revelation 20:10-15 (NLT)**

### The Fate for Christians:

14 "Don't let your hearts be troubled. Trust in God, and trust also in me. [2] There is more than enough room in my Father's home. [a] If this were not so, would I have told you that I am going to prepare a place for you? [b] [3] When everything is ready, I will come and get you, so that you will always be with me where I am. **(John 14:1-3) (NLT)**

### The Comfort of Christ's Coming

[13] But I do not want you to be ignorant, brethren, concerning those who have fallen asleep, lest you sorrow as others who have no hope. [14] For if we believe that Jesus died and rose again, even so God will bring with Him those who sleep in Jesus.

[15] For this we say to you by the word of the Lord, that we who are alive *and* remain until the coming of the Lord will by no means precede those who are asleep. [16] For the Lord Himself will descend from heaven with a shout, with the voice of an archangel, and with the trumpet of God. And the dead in Christ will rise first. [17] Then we who are alive *and* remain shall be caught up together with them in the clouds to meet the Lord in the air. And thus we shall always be with the Lord. [18] Therefore comfort one another with these words. **(1 Thessalonians 4:13-18)**

[18] I am the living one. I died, but look—I am alive forever and ever! And I hold the keys of death and the grave. **Revelation 1:18 (NLT)**

## Revelation 20 (KJV)

20 And I saw an angel come down from heaven, having the key of the bottomless pit and a great chain in his hand. [2] And he laid hold on the dragon, that old serpent, which is the Devil, and Satan, and bound him a thousand years, [3] And cast him into the bottomless pit, and shut him up, and set a seal upon him, that he should deceive the nations no more, till the thousand years should be fulfilled: and after that he must be loosed a little season.

[4] And I saw thrones, and they sat upon them, and judgment was given unto them: and I saw the souls of them that were beheaded for the witness of Jesus, and for the word of God, and which had not worshipped the beast, neither his image, neither had received his mark upon their foreheads, or in their hands; and they lived and reigned with Christ a thousand years.

[5] But the rest of the dead lived not again until the thousand years were finished. This is the first resurrection.

[6] Blessed and holy is he that hath part in the first resurrection: on such the second death hath no power, but they shall be priests of God and of Christ, and shall reign with him a thousand years.

[7] And when the thousand years are expired, Satan shall be loosed out of his prison,

[8] And shall go out to deceive the nations which are in the four quarters of the earth, Gog, and Magog, to gather them together to battle: the number of whom is as the sand of the sea.

[9] And they went up on the breadth of the earth, and compassed the camp of the saints about, and the beloved city: and fire came down from God out of heaven, and devoured them.

[10] And the devil that deceived them was cast into the lake of fire and brimstone, where the beast and the false prophet are, and shall be tormented day and night forever and ever.

[11] And I saw a great white throne, and him that sat on it, from whose face the earth and the heaven fled away; and there was found no place for them.

[12] And I saw the dead, small and great, stand before God; and the books were opened: and another book was opened, which is the book of life: and the dead were judged out of those things which were written in the books, according to their works.

[13] And the sea gave up the dead which were in it; and death and hell delivered up the dead which were in them: and they were judged every man according to their works.

[14] And death and hell were cast into the lake of fire. This is the second death. [15] And whosoever was not found written in the book of life was cast into the lake of fire.

> (For the weapons of our warfare are not carnal, but mighty through God to the pulling down of strong holds;) ⁵ Casting down imaginations, and every high thing that exalteth itself against the knowledge of God, and bringing into captivity every thought to the obedience of Christ; ⁶ And having in a readiness to revenge all disobedience, when your obedience is fulfilled. **2 Corinthians 10:4-6 (KJV)**

| God's Armor | Always Remember | The Word Of God |
|---|---|---|
| **Belt Of Truth** | The Good News Of Jesus Christ. The word of God is truth, The Holy Spirit is truth. | If we do not know the truth we will not know the counterfeit or the lie.<br><br>Whose minds the god of this age has blinded, who do not believe, lest the light of the gospel of the glory of Christ, who is the image of God, should shine on them. **(2 Corinthians 4:4)** |
| **Breastplate Of Righteousness** | The holy and perfect righteousness of Jesus in those who are "Born again" and filled with His Spirit | "Blessed are those who hunger and thirst for righteousness, for they shall be filled." **(Matt. 5:6)** My tongue shall speak of Your word, for all Your commandments are righteousness. **(Psalm 119:172)** |
| **Shoes Of Peace** | Share the Gospel Let the peace of God rule in your heart. | "How beautiful are the feet of them that preach the gospel of peace, and bring glad tidings of good things! *(Romans 10:15)* |
| **Shield Of Faith** | Read the bible Live by faith Pray daily | "Faith comes by hearing and hearing by the Word of God. **(Romans 10:17)** Thus we increase our faith by reading the Bible. Faith works in love **(Galatians 5:6)** |
| **Helmet on Salvation** | Salvation through Christ today and forever | Jesus said: "I am the way, the truth, and the life: no man cometh unto the Father But by me." **(John 14:6)** |
| **The Sword of the spirit: God's Word** | God's Word countering spiritual deception and accusations | ¹² For the word of God *is* living and powerful, and sharper than any two-edged sword, piercing even to the division of soul and spirit, and of joints and marrow, and is a discerner of the thoughts and intents of the heart. **(Hebrews 4:12)** |

# The Whole Armor of God

**Assignment:** God made it clear that we are not fighting against flesh-and-blood enemies but against the spiritual attacks of our enemy the devil. So when we are in arguments with family and friends or colleagues it's not always them! There are times people can say mean things to you because they are miserable and the devil will get in through anger, resentment, jealousy, pain, loss, greed, trauma, depression ect. Journal your thoughts and feelings.

We need to be aware that we do have an enemy the devil and he will use anyone who leaves a doorway open to get in and hurt you, friends, family, spouse, ect. A perfect example is Peter's love for Jesus, when Jesus is telling His disciples that He must go to Jerusalem, and that He would suffer to the point of death, but He would rise again on the third day. Peter tells Jesus that these things would not happen to Him. Peter loved Jesus and to think of Him dying was unacceptable. Jesus turned around and rebuked Peter. He looked at him and said, "Get thee behind me Satan."

Jesus rebuked Peter because his thoughts were in line with Satan's thoughts, even if it was done in love. Sin is committed under OUR FEELINGS and we find ourselves misguided. Satan followed Jesus around. Satan was present at the Last Supper when he used Judas to betray Jesus. Let's read the text before Jesus responded to the question asked of Him by the disciples, "Who will betray you?"

[26] Jesus responded, "It is the one to whom I give the bread I dip in the bowl." And when He had dipped it, He gave it to Judas, son of Simon Iscariot. [27] When Judas had eaten the bread, Satan entered into him. Then Jesus told him, "Hurry and do what you're going to do." **(John 13:26-27 NLT)**

**Action:** Get in prayer right now and ask God to reveal where the devil has a foothold in your life, where you seem to find yourself either in the same vicious cycle or ending up in places you do not want to be. Perhaps you are in the same relationship that ends badly over and over. Pray to God about the areas in your life that seem to not prosper. These attacks from the devil are what weaken our faith. Remember to cast down every high thing that exalted itself against the knowledge of God, and bring every thought to the obedience of Christ. This you can do by putting on the whole Armor of God and stay in prayer over these things on a daily basis.

Write down your dreams and desires that are under attack. Example: Who says you are not good enough or smart enough? Who said you're too young or too old? Who said you're too poor? Too dark? Too white? Who said you cannot finish school or get a degree? Who said it is too late? Who do you need to rebuke to move on in a positive direction? Make a list of what dreams and goals you have that continue to stagnate and let's talk to God in prayer about the desire for change, and for the Holy Spirit to guide you back to the path that God has always planned for you. Write a list of dreams that seem to be lost in battle. Example: a good marriage, serving in ministry, better education, healthy relationships, a specific job, mental health, physical health, healed addictions, a better relationship with your kids, parents, and siblings, having your own business. What negative thoughts are attacking your mind? Use your journal and prayer journal to write down your current battles. This will help you remember to stay in prayer daily about the obstacles we want God to remove.

1)_____

2)_____

3)_____

4)_____

5)_____

6)_____

7)_____

8)_____

9)_____

10)_____

11)_____

Journaling your thoughts and feelings helps you process events and release emotions. Journaling is a great tool for problem solving. Throughout this workbook you will find pages to journal your thoughts and dreams, and to document prayer requests and testimonials.

# JOURNAL

*Write down your thoughts and share them with the group.*

Date: _____

_____

_____

_____

_____

_____

_____

_____

_____

_____

_____

_____

_____

_____

_____

_____

_____

_____

_____

_____

# Biblical "911" Numbers

| | |
|---|---|
| When in sorrow | John 14, II Thessalonians 2:17, I Thess. 4:18 |
| When men fail you | Psalm 27 |
| If you want to be fruitful | John 15, Ephesians 5:17-18, Galatians 5:22-23 |
| When you have sinned | Psalm 42 and 51; I John 1:9, I John 2:1-2 |
| When you worry | Matthew 6:19-34, Philippians 4:4-9 |
| When you are in danger | Psalm 91, Psalm 33:20, Psalm 46:1-3 |
| When God seems far away | Psalm 139, Hebrews 10:19-22, James 4:8 |
| When your faith needs stirring | Hebrews 11, II Peter 1:1-11, I & II Timothy 1:12-14 |
| When you are lonely and fearful | Psalm 23 |
| When you grow bitter and critical | I Corinthians 13, Hebrews 12:12-15 |
| For Paul's secret to happiness | Colossians 3:12-17, Philippians 4 |
| For understanding of Christianity | II Corinthians 5:15-21, John 31-8,16, John 1:1-16 |
| When you feel down and out | Romans 8:31-39 |
| When you want peace and rest | Matthew 11:25-30, John 14:27 |
| When the world seems bigger than God | Psalm 90, Isaiah 40:21-26 |
| When you want Christian assurance | Romans 8:1-30, I John 5;11-13, John 5:24 |
| When you leave home for labor or travel | Psalm 121, Proverbs 3:5-7, Psalm 37:23-24 |
| When your prayers grow narrow or selfish | Psalm 67, Matthew 6:7-13, Eph. 6:18 |
| When you want courage for a task | Joshua 1, Ephesians 5:17-18, Phil. 4:13 |
| How to get along with others | Romans 12, Colossians 3:8-25 |
| If you are depressed | Psalm 27, Philippians 4, Nehemiah 8:10, John 15:1-11 |
| If your pocketbook is empty | Psalm 37 |
| If you are losing confidence in people | I Corinthians 13, Philippians 3:1-3 |
| If discouraged about your service | Psalm 126:5-6, Hebrews 6:10, Psalm 1:1-3 |
| If you are becoming proud | Psalm 19, I Peter 5:5-7, James 4:7-10 |
| For dealing with fear | Psalm 34:4-7, Hebrews 2:15-18, Hebrews 4:14-16 |
| For security and assurance | Psalm 121:1-8, John 10:27-30, I John 5:11-13 |
| For reassurance | Psalm 145:17-21, Romans 10:8-13, John 3:16 |

# 10 Addiction

> But as for me, I will look to the LORD, I will wait for the God of my salvation; my God will hear me.
> — Micah 7:7
>
> ©2006 GospelGifs

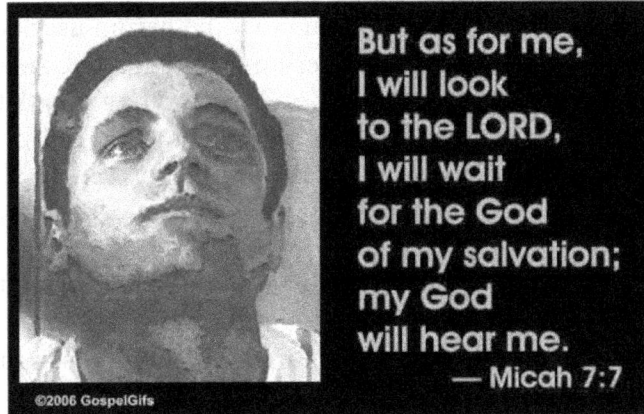

The temptations in your life are no different from what others experience. And God is faithful. He will not allow the temptation to be more than you can stand. When you are tempted, he will show you a way out so that you can endure. **(1 Corinthians 10:13 (NLT)**

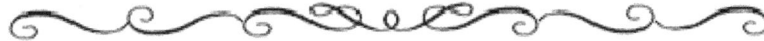

I am always honored and happy to talk to people who struggle with addiction as I do. I do not think people realize how deep emotional pain often causes our addictions, or how hurtful rather than helpful words of others often sustains our addiction. Some people repeatedly say things that are cruel. For example: No one wants to marry a fat person. You need to quit smoking, drinking, or using drugs. You're going to the casino again? That's 3 times this week. We become weary of people seeing only our faults and not our hearts. It is generally the criticisms of others that leads us into addiction in the first place, and that continued lack of feeling understood or cared about that keeps us dependent on whatever our addiction is that helps us cope.

We often do not know the truth of why we are bound, oppressed, and enslaved in our addictions. It doesn't matter how much education you have received from textbooks about addiction. It doesn't matter if someone has been clean and sober for many years. That is a great thing and gives us all hope, but what matters most in preventing or curing our addiction is knowing what has caused it in the first place. Most will not consider looking beyond the human experience for the truth about what makes us vulnerable to begin with.

We are all different and we all have different gifts but what I have seen in people who have addictions is that they generally seem to have a heart of gold. They are often very sensitive, loving and kind, caring people. They would give you their last dime. They are frequently gifted and talented, and with wonderful skills. I see the blessings on them because the Lord would show me how beautiful they truly are, despite the addiction.

Many people with addictions are among the most intelligent and have a calling in life that is greater than the addiction. Unfortunately the addiction often masks who they truly are, so you cannot see their beautiful sensitive hearts and great skills or gifts, you only see the addiction.

I know some people may say, "You mean to tell me that the heroin user down the street, who smells bad and is a thief, and keeps asking me for change every morning may be smarter than me? And has a calling from God that is bigger than the addiction?" YES I AM telling you that! It is what it is. People with addictions are frequently beautiful, loving, and highly intelligent people. When they are finally able to get help and get strong, and be free from the addiction, watch out! They can do all things through Christ Jesus who strengthens them!

When we talk about addictions we need to understand that addiction is not just alcohol and drugs. Once you have full knowledge of what an addiction is, you might realize that you may have one. Addictions can include, but are not limited to: drug abuse, alcohol, smoking, gambling, sex, pornography, exercise, food, dieting, computers, shopping, work, and video games.

We cannot continue to judge people by how long they were enslaved to their addiction. Let's celebrate when they are strong and whole. People that remember the old me sometimes remind me of what I did way back when, but that girl died. I am a new creation in Christ Jesus, and they missed the funeral when I got saved and baptized. Addiction is a trap from the enemy - the devil. God warned us in this text:

[34] But take heed to yourselves *and* be on your guard, lest your hearts be overburdened *and* depressed (weighed down) with the giddiness *and* headache and nausea of self-indulgence, drunkenness, and worldly worries *and* cares pertaining to the business of this life, and lest that day come upon you suddenly like a trap *or* a noose; Amplified Bible **(Luke 21:34) (Amp)**

### Why would God say to take heed: be on guard? Guard from what? A trap from who? And why you?

If you read the text again in **Luke 21:34** it says **worldly worries** *and* cares **pertaining to** the **business of this life,** and lest that day come upon you **suddenly like a trap**.

People that have a heart of gold often care more than others understand. We say to them, "Why are you so worried about it? It is not your problem." People that care more than others will often suffer more than others, and the devil will use that as a way in. These types of people normally will have trouble sleeping because they care too much, love too much, and tend to forget about themselves. Many get taken advantage of because they are multi-talented and kind, and their heart gets overburdened, causing them to become unhappy and depressed. Others have been traumatized or have shame from hidden secrets of being abused, raped, molested or have abandonment issues that may be too painful to share. Too often having an addiction can be one's temporary answer to feeling better about life and the inner pain that comes with it.

The devil is going to attack wherever you are vulnerable and weak. You must constantly be on guard to prevent his attack. Do a careful inventory of what drama surrounds you, what thoughts and actions plague you and weigh you down, what keeps happening constantly to depress you or make you sad, anxious and unhappy. Pray about these burdens and ask God to give you strength and courage to fight your way through them, overcoming these trials and rising above them to be everything God has equipped you to be for His divine purpose!

Genetics can cause a tendency toward addiction for some individuals. Social media often define this type of addiction as a disease. But only our Redeemer has the key to close that Gateway to addiction, regardless of how you came to addiction or what your genetics are. Once the door to addiction is opened, He is the only one that can help - our creator God, who knows all and is all, who loves you unconditionally and can help you through anything and everything.

God said, "Watch out, the devil comes to steal, kill and destroy." And we see how addiction has killed people physically and spiritually. The devil also steals by taking kids away from their parents due to the addiction trap of the enemy. Yes, a person's free will may have played a part, but the devil leads us to believe there will be no lasting consequences for our actions, he deludes our thinking so that we don't believe we might lose our children, alienate our families and friends, and even eventually ruin our health or cause our untimely death. People who are loving and kind, and caring can make a huge Impact for the Kingdom of God, and the devil especially does not wish for these type of people to be strong and well, and make that Impact for God to happen.

If you're in your addiction you cannot function to do the great things God has designed you to do consistently. So the skills and the talents cannot be used to the degree they were originally intended. This is just another way the devil will attack. He can use you for his purpose and in exchange you feed your addiction - until physical death, and even spiritual death, because using drugs keeps our focus away from God, so spiritually and physically we're slowly dying. Even though your spirit cries out for help, it is **trapped** and out of control from addiction.

Addiction is not a simple fix because it is a spiritual battle as well as a physical one. If we only look at it in a physical way, we can never get the help we really need. We are getting a 'bunk' recovery like 'bunk' weed. We need the strength and endurance that God will give. God has the answer and He is the only way. Let's go back to the text in the beginning:

The temptations in your life are no different from what others experience. And God is faithful. He will not allow the temptation to be more than you can stand. When you are tempted, he will show you a way out so that you can endure. **(1 Corinthians 10:13 (NLT)**

God says your struggle is no different from what others experience. That is why we cannot judge. **God will give you a way out.** I love the way he put it in text:

Do not judge *and* criticize *and* condemn others, so that you may not be judged *and* criticized *and* condemned yourselves. For just as you judge *and* criticize *and* condemn others, you will be judged *and* criticized *and* condemned, and in accordance with the measure you [use to] deal out to others, it will be dealt out again to you. [3] Why do you stare from without at the very small particle that is in your brother's Eye but do not come aware of *and* consider the beam of timber that is in your own eye? **(Matthew 7:1-3) (AMP)**

The first thing you have to do is **get honest**. Admit to God how you know now that you were under attack, and by your choices you now have a serious uncontrollable addiction that has resulted in ongoing problems in your life. Admit that you want and need God's help and guidance so you can break free from being a slave to your addiction, and get back on the path God originally planned for you.

The key to true recovery is standing on faith and the word of God. He said He will give you the way out, which means you must trust in God because he has your key. You must not be prideful. Ask for the help that you need and start doing the legwork by talking to an addiction specialist in your area. They will help you put together a treatment plan. God will restore what was taken.

[3] He restored my soul: he leadeth me in the paths of righteousness for his name's sake.
**(Psalm 23:3) (KJV)**

And just know your addiction does not take away from who you truly are, regardless of how you feel you are beautiful! You are great! You are worth it! And most of all God loves you. He cares. No one is perfect and we all have made mistakes. We all have regrets, but to love ourselves and others is so important in our recovery! It is a process. Just know you are loved, truly, by God. I love this text:

And I am convinced that nothing can ever separate us from God's love. Neither death nor life, neither angels nor demons, neither our fears for today nor our worries about tomorrow—not even the powers of hell can separate us from God's love. [39] No power in the sky above or in the earth below—indeed, nothing in all creation will ever be able to separate us from the love of God that is revealed in Christ Jesus our Lord. **(Romans 8:38-39) (NLT)**

Remember The Bible says that, "The Holy Spirit helps when we are powerless. Likewise the Spirit helps us in our weakness. Since we do not know what to pray for as we ought, but the Spirit himself intercedes for us with groans too deep for words." **(Romans 8:26) (ESV)** In order to be filled by the Holy Spirit, you first must have faith, as you receive Jesus Christ by faith. Second, you must surrender your life. Third, you must confess your sins and repent.

# Meet Lee-Anna

Hi there my name is Lee-Anna and I'm the pen-pal coordinator for Sacramento Prison Aglow. I have been a Pen-Pal coordinator for just about 10 years now. I write the men and women in the prisons and jails encouraging them with God's word. I use to average about 3-5 letters a week and now I get 8-15 letters a week and I write each one of them. Now we get letters from all over from men and women in prisons and jails and 99% of the time people are asking me for this book "A Turn In My Belly" so I am happy to have the opportunity to send you this book.

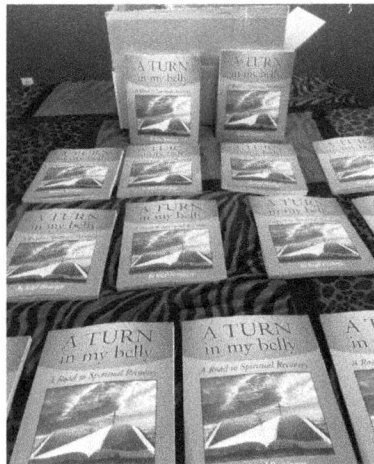

You now have another tool you can use along with your bible. Different people have written me saying there doing group Bible studies with this book in the prisons and jails how awesome is that!

God is doing great things through this book "A Turn In My Belly"

I thank you for reaching out and asking for materials that will help you grow closer to God. I am honored to be able to help you along your journey and May you be blessed and stay encouraged. I want to leave you with this prayer.

Take care. Your sister in the Lord Lee-Anna

## A PRAYER FOR WHEN YOU'RE WAITING ON THE LORD

Father,
Forgive me for all my doubts, worries, and fears.
Forgive me for my impatience as I wait in this place.
Forgive me for questioning the story you've written for me.
I believe, help me in my unbelief!
Help me to remember that it is good to wait for you.
Grant me the joy that comes from knowing you .
Fill my heart with gospel joy.
Amen.

iBelieve.com

# Take an Addiction Test

## The CAGE Test for Alcohol Addiction

This simple test is surprisingly accurate. Answer yes or no to each question.

1. Have you ever felt you should **C**ut down on your drinking?
2. Have you ever been **A**nnoyed when people have commented on your drinking?
3. Have you ever felt **G**uilty or bad about your drinking?
4. Have you ever had a drink an **E**ye opener first thing in the morning to steady your nerves or get rid of a hangover?

**Your score:**
Score one point for each yes answer. A total score of 2 or higher indicates a problem with alcohol.

If you scored 1, there is an 80% chance you're addicted to alcohol.
If you scored 2, there is an 89% chance you're addicted to alcohol.
If you scored 3, there is a 99% chance you're addicted to alcohol.
If you scored 4, there is a 100% chance you're addicted to alcohol.

## The Modified CAGE Test for All Addictions

Most self-test questionnaires apply to alcohol addiction, but can be easily adapted to any addiction.

1. Have you ever felt you should **C**ut down your use of drugs?
2. Have you ever been **A**nnoyed when people have commented on your use?
3. Have you ever felt **G**uilty or badly about your use?
4. Have you ever used drugs to **E**ase withdrawal symptoms, or to avoid feeling low after using?

The CAGE questionnaire was developed by Dr. John Ewing, founding director of the Bowles Center for Alcohol Studies, University of North Carolina at Chapel Hill. CAGE is an internationally used assessment instrument for identifying problems with alcohol. 'CAGE' is an acronym formed from the italicized letters in the questionnaire (cut-annoyed-guilty-eye).

The exact wording that can be used in research studies can be found in: JA Ewing (1984) 'Detecting Alcoholism: The CAGE Questionnaire', *Journal of the American Medical Association* 252: 1905-1907

# Am I a Food Addict?

**To find out, answer the following questions as honestly as you can.**

1. Have you ever wanted to stop eating and found you just couldn't?
2. Do you think about food or your weight constantly?
3. Do you find yourself attempting one diet or food plan after another, with no lasting success?
4. Do you binge and then "get rid of the binge" through vomiting, exercise, laxatives, or other forms of purging?
5. Do you eat differently in private than you do in front of other people?
6. Has a doctor or a family member ever approached you with concern about your eating habits or weight?
7. Do you eat large quantities of food at one time (binge)?
8. Is your weight problem due to your "nibbling" all day long?
9. Do you eat to escape from your feelings?
10. Do you eat when you're not hungry?
11. Have you ever discarded food, only to retrieve and eat it later?
12. Do you eat in secret?
13. Do you fast or severely restrict your food intake?
14. Have you ever stolen other people's food?
15. Have you ever hidden food to make sure you have "enough"?
16. Do you feel driven to exercise excessively to control your weight?
17. Do you obsessively calculate the calories you've burned against the calories you've eaten?
18. Do you frequently feel guilty or ashamed about what you've eaten?
19. Are you waiting for your life to begin "when you lose the weight"?
20. Do you feel hopeless about your relationship with food?

If you answered yes to any of the above questions, then you may be a food addict. You are not alone. There is help for all addictions.

# Are you a compulsive gambler?

Answer all 20 questions below Most victims of compulsive gambling will answer "yes" to at least seven of these questions.

| | | | |
|----|---|---|---|
| 1. | Did you ever lose time from work or school due to gambling? | Yes | No |
| 2. | Has gambling ever made your home life unhappy? | Yes | No |
| 3. | Did gambling affect your reputation? | Yes | No |
| 4. | Have you ever felt remorse after gambling? | Yes | No |
| 5. | Did you ever gamble to get money with which to pay debts or otherwise solve financial difficulties? | Yes | No |
| 6. | Did gambling cause a decrease in your ambition or efficiency? | Yes | No |
| 7. | After losing did you feel you must return as soon as possible and win back your losses? | Yes | No |
| 8. | After a win did you have a strong urge to return and win more? | Yes | No |
| 9. | Did you often gamble until your last dollar was gone? | Yes | No |
| 10. | Did you ever borrow to finance your gambling? | Yes | No |
| 11. | Have you ever sold anything to finance gambling? | Yes | No |
| 12. | Were you reluctant to use "gambling money" for normal expenditures? | Yes | No |
| 13. | Did gambling make you careless of the welfare of yourself or your family? | Yes | No |
| 14. | Did you ever gamble longer than you had planned? | Yes | No |
| 15. | Have you ever gambled to escape worry, trouble, boredom or loneliness? | Yes | No |
| 16. | Have you ever committed, or considered committing, an illegal act to finance gambling? | Yes | No |
| 17. | Did gambling cause you to have difficulty in sleeping? | Yes | No |
| 18. | Do arguments, disappointments or frustrations create within you an urge to gamble? | Yes | No |
| 19. | Did you ever have an urge to celebrate any good fortune by a few hours of gambling? | Yes | No |
| 20. | Have you ever considered self-destruction or suicide as a result of your gambling? | Yes | No |

# Support Groups

- Alcoholics Anonymous (AA) (aa.org)
- Celebrate Recovery is a Christian based 12 step program. Like Alcoholics Anonymous and Narcotics Anonymous Celebrate Recovery group meetings can be located in most cities throughout the United States. (www.celebraterecovery.com)
- Al-Anon.org (al-anon.org) For family members of addicts.
- Cocaine Anonymous (CA) (ca.org)
- Crystal Meth Anonymous (CMA) (crystalmeth.org)
- Food Addicts in Recovery Anonymous (FA) (foodaddicts.org)
- Gamblers Anonymous (GA) (gamblersanonymous.org)
- Narcotics Anonymous (NA) (na.org)
- Nar-Anon (nar-anon.org) For family members of addicts.
- Nicotine Anonymous (nicotine-anonymous.org)
- Marijuana Anonymous (marijuana-anonymous.org)
- Methadone Anonymous (methadoneanonymous.info)
- S-Anon (sanon.org)
- Sexaholics Anonymous (sa.org)
- Sex and Love Addicts Anonymous (SLAA) (slaafws.org)
- Women for Sobriety (WFS) (womenforsobriety.org)
- XA Speakers (xa-speakers.org) A collection of recordings from speaker meetings, conventions and workshops of 12-step groups.
- 12 Steps (12step.org) Resources for all 12 step programs. It contains an in-depth discussion and forum on the 12 steps.
- 12steptreatmentcentres.com   A list of 12 Step treatment centers around the world.

# 11. Will We See Our Pets In Heaven

<sup>10</sup> The Godly care for their animals, but the wicked are always cruel.
**(Proverbs 12:10) (NLT)**


A lot of us always wonder about our pets and will we see them in heaven. I believe we will. Especially when we read the text **"For the life of every living thing is in his hand."** God is merciful and loving and our pets and animals are such a big part of our life here on earth. I feel God has a plan for them as well. When Noah built the ark, God included the animals. He wanted us to have them with us, including our pets. God had a purpose for each one of them:

<sup>19</sup> Bring a pair of every kind of animal—a male and a female—into the boat with you to keep them alive during the flood. <sup>20</sup> Pairs of every kind of bird, **and every kind of animal**, and every kind of small animal that scurries along the ground, **will come to you to be kept alive**. (Genesis 6:19-22) (NLT)


Some of us have had our pets for many years. They become a part of our family and when they pass away we are devastated, just as if they were a family member or friend, because they mean that much to us. We love our furry friends and we treat them as if they were our children. Some of us prefer the company of our pets more than people and have to depend on them just as much as a person. Think about how dogs are able to be trained to become guide dogs for the blind, or as a companion for the lonely, homeless or elderly. We call them service dogs, watchdogs or herding animals that help on the farm. We see cats as companions. Researchers say that cats alleviate stress and anxiety, and potentially reduce the risk of heart attacks in humans by 30 percent. Animals of all kinds bring us hope, joy, and most of all un-conditional love. Every pet, and every animal have a purpose.

God kept all kinds of animals from the beginning, because God loves them too. He wants us to treat them as He did from the beginning. He made sure they had food and shelter, and has put us in charge of animals to look after them. The reason why we fall in love with animals is because God intended for us to love and care for them.

It is God who gives them life, and yes they are in God's hands. God is love, so I am confident when saying our pets that have passed from this life are also with our creator. Let's read the text:

**Revelation 19:11** [11]"I saw heaven standing open and there before me was a white horse."

So we know there are animals in heaven. And God told Noah to bring a pair of every kind of animal because they were important to God. That is why they are with us, because they are a part of God's plan here on earth. Anything and everything we see that has breath was created by God and we have to trust in God that He has a plan for all His creation. We should value God's creatures as he valued us. God never created throwaway pets. What is amazing is that in the Bible it is written how there are pets and other animals that know Jesus. Read the text:

(**Revelations 5:13**) And then I heard **every creature in heaven and on earth and under the earth and in the sea**. They sang:

"Blessing and honor and glory and power
Belong to the one sitting on the throne
And to the Lamb forever and ever."

We need to be careful how we treat everyone, including our pets and other animals. They all belong to God.

[10] For all the animals of the forest are mine, and I own the cattle on a thousand hills. I know every bird on the mountains, **and all the animals of the field are mine**. (**Psalm 50:10-11**) (**NLT**)

We tend to forget that everything belongs to God and we are so very fortunate to be able to experience the close relationships that we have with our pets. We must treat all living things with respect and know that God watches how we treat them. Thank you God for our pets that are still with us, and for those that are with You!

# 12. Children Are A Blessing

Jesus said, "Permit the children to come to me, and do not stop them; for it is to such as these that the kingdom of God belongs.
Luke 18:16

©2006 GospelGifs

"Children are a gift from the LORD; they are a reward from him." **(Psalm 127:3) (NLT)**

Even our children belong to God. They are a gift from God and a blessing. There are people with children that do not realize God has a plan for your kids and has left you instructions on raising them.

## Children and Parents

**<u>Children, obey your parents because you belong to the Lord</u>**, for this is the right thing to do. "Honor your father and mother." This is the first commandment with a promise: [3] If you honor your father and mother, "things will go well for you, and you will have a long life on the earth."

[4] Fathers, do not provoke your children to anger by the way you treat them. Rather, bring them up with the discipline and instruction that comes from the Lord. **(Ephesians 6) (NLT)**

I was the third child of four. My mom did the best to raise us on her own. My dad was an absentee father, at least in our household. He had another family that he took care of and forgot about us, leaving my mom to fend for herself and us kids. My mom always worked two jobs. She worked day and night to make sure we had what was needed. I never remember my dad ever coming around except this one time when I was in … maybe 4th or 5th grade. He came by and all my brothers, and my sister, visited with him briefly.

I remember he told me he was going to be back to bring me a bike so I could ride with my friends. I was so excited that I told my friends, but he never showed up again. I never forgot the way I felt when my friends sat and waited with me for my dad to come with this great bike. I just remember my friends rode away because the sun went down and it was time for them to get home before dark.

Then when I was in my thirties I got a phone call that my dad was dying and was diagnosed with throat cancer. They did not expect him to live more than two weeks. I remember I took my best friend with me to visit my dad because I really did not know him. He was a stranger to me. I just felt that regardless, he was my dad and he was dying. I had better go see him. My dad had many children from different wives, but I noticed no one really came around. He had been divorced and was drinking heavily. He was an alcoholic and very abusive.

I had just moved to Sacramento, California. My dad lived about an hour and a half away from where I lived, but he had decided to try this new cancer treatment, which was given in Sacramento. There was a chance this treatment might save his life. In exchange they would house him across from the hospital but he would need someone to live there with him during the treatment. Since I lived in Sacramento I told my dad I would be there and look after him along with my best friend, because you have to remember that even though he was my dad, he was a stranger and I did not know him.

I was so happy thinking maybe now I can get to know my dad, so every day I would get up and help him get prepared to go to the doctor for his radiation and chemotherapy. He also was on a feeding tube. He would not talk much and when he got home he would quickly go into his room and shut the door. I felt sad because we were so disconnected, but he was my dad. I remember how uncomfortable it was when the nurse would tell my dad, "Your daughter is such a blessing, how she makes an attempt to be here with you at every appointment." He would smile. I remember thinking, "I do not even know this man."

What was really strange is that I had no anger against him. I really wanted him to recover. He never did. However he did live longer than the doctors had said he would in the beginning. Instead of the two weeks they predicted, through the care and support of the cancer study medical professionals, he lived about 2 months. I just remember how he suffered due to the cancer and how I still did not get to know him as much as I would of liked to.

I do remember my car would not start one morning. He came out of his room and showed me how to clean the terminals on my battery. The car started right up. I learned that my dad enjoyed playing dominoes. I remember my sister, stepbrother, and I challenged him in dominoes and it was fun. And my dad liked sherbet. What I remember most of all is that he read the paper every morning.

I learned some things about my dad that I did not know, even though in the beginning he was very sick. After he died I thought about how hard it must have been for him to see me there every day taking care of him, when he never took care of me. He missed my wedding, birthdays, graduations, and a baby's first step. I never looked at the situation through his eyes. The guilt and shame he must have felt, on top being sick. My father must have cried out to God in his need, because I never wanted to leave my dad's side.

I could not depend on an absentee father, but he was able to depend on God because it was God who allowed me to be there for my dad. Even though I did not have as close of a relationship with God as I do now, I remember a part of me would always say that regardless of my dad not being there for me, he is still my dad and he needs me.

I was honoring my dad because God put it in my heart to honor him, and because of what I was taught as a child from my mother. The best inheritance you could give your kids is to tell them the truth about Jesus Christ and his teachings. Then your child will make Godly decisions and do the right thing regardless of what people say or feel. They will do what God would of wanted them to do.

[4] Fathers, do not provoke your children to anger by the way you treat them. Rather, bring them up with the discipline and instruction that comes from the Lord. **(Ephesians 6:4) (NLT)**

I did not know anything about my father's relationship with God. He never told me about God or ever prayed with me, or taught me about God's instructions. Yet I knew God was with me.

<sup>18</sup> No, I will not abandon you as orphans—I will come to you. **(John 14:18) (NLT)**

God said he would not abandon us as orphans so there are no illegitimate kids, just illegitimate parents. Even though my father was not there for me, I still consider it a reward for Him, and a blessing, to be there for my dad's situation. God is great and God is good all the time, even when we do not deserve what He gives us, He still blesses us. I do not have any children, but when I have an opportunity to be around kids or younger adults I make sure I show and lead with a good example. We are not perfect but we should do our best. Children are our future and whether they had an absentee parent or even if they had both parents, one still can be an 'absentee parent' if that parent did not spend time with their child. God is still with us and will show us the way. God is not going to change the plans He had for us because of human error.

I hear people say they will let their kids decide what religion to choose when they get older. Satan loves this idea because he gets to raise them. He is given access to by the parent's free will. I am glad my mom raised me with a spiritual foundation, knowing there is a God, and prayed over me, and for me, at a young age. I thank my Grandmother for laying the foundation for my mother, so she would have the knowledge of God and his precious son Jesus Christ. It is not too late if you are a parent and your kids were taken away, or the relationship is not there due to circumstances. Pray for your children anyway. God knows we make mistakes and He know's when we have a change of heart. If you are in your kids' life, evaluate what you're teaching them. Are you living by the same examples? God wants us united, not divided. Whatever the circumstances are let go and let God into your life and your kids' life because we all belong to God first!

We Worship Jesus Together

# Spiritual Gifts

Now, dear brothers and sisters, regarding your question about the special abilities the Spirit gives us. I don't want you to misunderstand this. You know that when you were still pagans, you were led astray and swept along in worshiping speechless idols. So I want you to know that no one speaking by the Spirit of God will curse Jesus, and no one can say Jesus is Lord, except by the Holy Spirit.

<u>There are different kinds of spiritual gifts, but the same Spirit is the source of them all.</u> There are different kinds of service, but we serve the same Lord. God works in different ways, but it is the same God who does the work in all of us.

A spiritual gift is given to each of us so we can help each other. To one person the Spirit gives the ability to give wise advice, to another the same Spirit gives a message of special knowledge. The same Spirit gives great faith to another, and to someone else the one Spirit gives the gift of healing. He gives one person the power to perform miracles, and another the ability to prophesy. He gives someone else the ability to discern whether a message is from the Spirit of God or from another spirit. Still another person is given the ability to speak in unknown languages, while another is given the ability to interpret what is being said. It is the one and only Spirit who distributes all these gifts. He alone decides which gift each person should have. **(1 Corinthians 12:1-11) (NLT)**

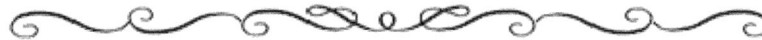

The above scripture confirms that God gives each and every one of us special abilities. These are spiritual gifts that will give us special powers which can work in a capacity that another may not have. Not everyone can have the same abilities because these spiritual gifts are not taught. They cannot be learned; it is a gift. Some of us will share the same gift. God wants each and every one of us to know that we have been given a spiritual gift.

People started to worship other Gods/Idols and were led astray from God. Some had even gotten into superstition and witchcraft. The true spirit of God would not have made these choices and the ones who continue to do these things do not have the true spirit of God. No man could say Jesus is Lord, but only by the Holy Spirit. All of the spiritual gifts, which I will explain in detail, come from the same Spirit (God). Even though we have different spiritual gifts and we serve differently we still serve the same God. Each spiritual gift works differently and God designed each one for the perfecting of the saints, for the work of the ministry, and the edifying of the body of Christ.

Our spiritual gifts should help one another on an everyday basis. This is why we need to be united in our efforts. We were never designed to be a lone ranger. There are some things one cannot do that someone else can help with, so it is important to get along and work as one body. Just think if we were all patients but no one had a gift of healing, we would just be sick people watching each other die. God is great and gave us spiritual abilities and when these gifts are working as God intended, everyone benefits. It is so important to recognize what your gifts are because when you are operating in your God-given gift, you are running at your best – you are in sync.

Spiritual Gifts

**Word of Wisdom** This gift is knowing what to say in a way one can better understand. To share the word of God and messages in a way that it will shed light on events in people's lives and give a better understanding. God will give you the right words to speak, especially in difficult circumstances when you are afraid and unsure. This gift also speaks out what the true will of God is for applying to your life. It is giving wise advice.

"When you are arrested, don't worry about how to respond or what to say. God will give you the right words at the right time. For it is not you who will be speaking—it will be the Spirit of your Father speaking through you." **(Matthew 10:18-20) (NLT)**

**Word of Knowledge** This gift is having a supernatural understanding. The ability to explain lessons from God in a way others can understand. It is having information you could not have known on your own; a special message given from God. It is the ability to analyze and lay out the truth for the benefit of others. God answers your innermost questions. It is to instruct, advise and warn.

"And I myself also am persuaded of you, my brethren, that ye also are full of goodness, filled with all knowledge, able also to admonish one another." **(Romans 15:14) (NKJV)**

**The Gift of Prophecy** This gift is seen in pastors and also people who do not pastor a church. People with this gift will minister and declare the divine will of God and to speak out the truth of Jesus Christ. God will use them to equip the saints for growth by an inspired foretelling. They will be able to build people up spiritually and strengthen people by giving encouragement, comfort, and support. God will use someone with this gift to advise or caution people.

"But one who prophesies strengthens others, encourages them, and comforts them."
**(1 Corinthians 14:3) (NLT)**

**The Gift of Faith** This gift does not allow human thoughts or weaknesses to overshadow the divine will and power of God. Someone with this gift has a clear understanding of God's authority. They will follow God even though they do not know where they are going. They know nothing is impossible for God so they come to Him with patience and persistence, calling out to God. It is the spiritual ability to trust in God, and knowing the true power of God.

And when Jesus was entered into Capernaum, there came unto him a centurion, beseeching him,[6] And saying, Lord, my servant lieth at home sick of the palsy, grievously tormented.[7] And Jesus saith unto him, I will come and heal him.[8] The centurion answered and said, Lord, I am not worthy that thou shouldest come under my roof: but speak the word only, and my servant shall be healed.[9] For I am a man under authority, having soldiers under me: and I say to this man, Go, and he goeth; and to another, Come, and he cometh; and to my servant, Do this, and he doeth it.[10] When Jesus heard it, he marvelled, and said to them that followed, Verily I say unto you, I have not found so great faith, no, not in Israel. **(Matthew 8:5-10)(KJV)**

**The Gift of Healing** This is the gift of supernatural healing without human aid, which symbolizes how believers can be channels/vessels of Divine Power, and their healings can be the work of the Holy Spirit. Those with the gift of healing trust God to heal and restore the sick, and they will pray in faith for those in need. People with this gift will see someone healed when God uses them, since healing is something that God alone decides to do and at what time. This gift includes the ability to sense when God is prompting you to pray this kind of prayer.

[17] And these signs shall follow them that believe; In my name shall they cast out devils; they shall speak with new tongues;[18] They shall take up serpents; and if they drink any deadly thing, it shall not hurt them; they shall lay hands on the sick, and they shall recover. **(Mark 16:17-18)(KJV)**

**The Gift of Miracles** God will use certain individuals to be a part of a miracle and cause something unexplainable that supersedes natural laws and thinking. It is the ability to pray, in faith, specifically for God's supernatural intervention into an impossible situation. A doctor examines a man who has pain in the back of his head. The doctor takes x-rays and finds out the man has a large tumor. After praying the doctor does a follow up and the tumor is completely gone, yet he has previously taken pictures of a large tumor. God works miracles, signs, and wonders through this gift.

John said to Jesus, "Teacher, we saw someone using your name to cast out demons, but we told him to stop because he wasn't in our group."[39] "Don't stop him!" Jesus said. "No one who performs a miracle in my name will soon be able to speak evil of me. [40] Anyone who is not against us is for us. **(Mark 9:38-40)(NLT)**

**The Gift of Discerning of Spirits** Discerning of spirits is a gift given by the Holy Spirit. This gift can enable you to discern if something is coming from God or not. God will supernaturally give you the power to detect that something does not line up and you will be able to tell if a spiritual manifestation is from God or not. Discern means to see or perceive. This gift can be used to fully expose what is really going on and operating behind the scenes with someone. It is the spiritual ability to distinguish between good and evil, right and wrong

As we were on our way to the place of prayer, we were met by a slave girl who was possessed by a spirit of divination [claiming to foretell future events and to discover hidden knowledge], and she brought her owners much gain by her fortunetelling. She kept following Paul and [the rest of] us, shouting loudly, These men are the servants of the Most High God! They announce to you the way of salvation! And she did this for many days. Then Paul, being sorely annoyed *and* worn out, turned and said to the spirit within her, I charge you in the name of Jesus Christ to come out of her! And it came out that very moment. **(Acts 16:16-19) (Amplified Bible)**

**The Gift of Tongues** This gift from the Holy Spirit is a spiritual language that edifies the one who has the gift and will build them up. This gift cannot be taught; it is given, and the one speaking in a spiritual language may not understand what they are saying unless they can also "Interpret" or someone "Interprets" for them, someone who has the gift of "Interpretation of Tongues."

No more than two or three should speak in tongues. They must speak one at a time, and someone must interpret what they say. But if no one is present who can interpret, they must be silent in your church meeting and speak in tongues to God privately. Let two or three people prophesy, and let the others evaluate what is said **(1 Corinthians 14:27-29) (NLT)**

For if you have the ability to speak in tongues, you will be talking only to God, since people won't be able to understand you. You will be speaking by the power of the Spirit, but it will all be mysterious. **(1 Corinthians 14:9) (NLT)**

**The Gift of Interpretation of Tongues** This gift is the ability to give or provide the meaning of what is being said. To have understanding of a language that you did not learn. This is a gift from God; to interpret an unknown language.

# A LIST OF
# SPIRITUAL GIFTS
### (Mainly from 1 Cor. 12, Eph. 4, Rom. 12)

**ADMINISTRATION:** 1 Cor. 12:28 (This is sometimes called "**Organization**") The ability to recognize the gifts of others and recruit them to a ministry. The ability to organize and manage people, resources, and time for effective ministry.

**APOSTLE:** 1 Cor. 12:28 The ability to start new churches/ventures and oversee their development.

**CRAFTSMANSHIP:** Exodus 30:22-25, 31:3, 2 Chron. 34:9-13, Acts 18:2-3 The ability to use one's hands, thoughts and mind to further the kingdom of God through artistic, creative means. People with this gift may also serve to lead others in forming their abilities in this area.

**CREATIVE COMMUNICATION:** Deut. 31:22, 1 Sam. 16:16, 1 Chron. 16:41, 2 Chron. 5:12, 34:12, Psalm 150 (Sometimes narrowly defined as **Music**) The ability to communicate Gods' truth through a variety of art forms.

**DISCERNMENT:** 1 Cor. 12:10 The ability to distinguish between the spirit of truth and the spirit of error. The ability to detect inconsistencies in another's life and confront in love.

**ENCOURAGEMENT:** Rom. 12:8 (This is sometimes called "**Exhortation**") The ability to motivate God's people to apply and act on biblical principles, especially when they are discouraged or wavering in their faith. The ability to bring out the best in others and challenge them to develop their potential.

**EVANGELISM:** Eph. 4:11-14 The ability to communicate the Good News of Jesus Christ to unbelievers in a positive, non-threatening way. The ability to sense opportunities to share Christ and lead people to respond with faith.

**FAITH:** 1 Cor. 12:9 The ability to trust God for what cannot be seen and to act on God's promise, regardless of what the circumstances indicate. The willingness to risk failure in pursuit of a God-given vision, expecting God to handle the obstacles.

**GIVING:** Rom. 12:8 The ability to generously contribute material resources and/or money so that the Body may grow and be strengthened. The ability to manage money so it may be given to support the ministry of others.

**HEALING:** 1 Cor. 12:9, 28 The ability to pray, in faith, specifically for people who need physical, emotional, or spiritual healing and see God answer. The ability to sense when God is prompting you to pray this kind of prayer.

**HOSPITALITY:** Romans 12:9-13, 1 Peter 4:9-10 The ability to make others, especially strangers, feel warmly welcomed, accepted, and comfortable in the church family. The ability to coordinate factors that promote fellowship.

**INTERCESSION/PRAYER:** Luke 22:41-44, Acts 12:12, Col. 1:9-12, 4:12-13, 1 Timothy 2:1-2, James 5:14-16 The ability to pray for extended periods of time on a regular basis and see frequent .And specific answers to prayer, to a degree much greater than that which is experienced by most Christians.

**KNOWLEDGE**: (Word of Knowledge): 1 Cor. 12:8, Acts 5:1-11, 2 Cor. 11:6, Col. 2:2-3 The ability to bring truth to the body through revelation or biblical insight.

**LEADERSHIP:** Rom. 12:8    The ability to clarify and communicate the purpose and direction ("vision") of a ministry in a way that attracts others to get involved. The ability to motivate others

**MERCY:** Rom. 12:8  The ability to manifest practical, compassionate, cheerful love toward suffering   members of the Body of Christ.

**MIRACLES:** 1 Cor. 12:10, 28  The ability to pray, in faith, specifically for God's supernatural intervention into an impossible situation and see God answer. The ability to sense when God is prompting you to pray this kind of prayer.

**MISSIONARY:**  Acts 8:4, 13:2-3, 22:21, Romans 10:15, 1 Cor. 9:19-23  The ability to  Minister with whatever other spiritual gifts one has in a second culture.

**PASTORING:**  Eph. 4:11-14  (This is sometimes called "**Shepherding**")  The ability to care for  the spiritual needs of a group of believers and equip them for ministry. The ability to nurture a small  group in spiritual growth and assume responsibility for their welfare.

**PREACHING:**  Rom. 12:6  (This is sometimes called "**Prophecy**") The ability to publicly  Communicate God's Word in an inspired way that convinces unbelievers and both challenges and  comforts believers. The ability to persuasively declare God's will.

**SERVICE:** Rom. 12:7 (Often described under **Helps)**  The ability to recognize unmet needs in the church family, and take the initiative to provide practical assistance quickly, cheerfully, and without a need for recognition.

**TEACHING:**   1Cor. 12:23, Eph. 4:11-14 The ability to educate God's people by clearly explaining  and applying the Bible in a way that causes them to learn. The ability to equip and train other believers for ministry.

**TONGUES/LANGUAGES** (ALSO Interpretation):  Mark 16:17, Acts 2:1-13, 10:44- 46, 19:1-7   The ability to speak a spontaneous message from God in an unknown language that is then made known to the church through the gift of interpretation.

**WISDOM:** 1 Cor. 12:8  The ability to understand God's perspective on life situations and share those  insights in a simple, understandable way. The ability to explain what to do and how to do it.

| My Top 3 or 4 Spiritual Gifts from Assessment | My Perceived Spiritual Gifts from definitions above | Spiritual Gifts Observed in me by others |
|---|---|---|
| 1._____ | 1._____ | 1._____ |
| 2._____ | 2._____ | 2._____ |
| 3._____ | 3._____ | 3._____ |
| 4._____ | | |

**(This information is used by permission from the website http://www.oaklandumc.com)**

# Spiritual Gifts Survey

The following is an evaluation designed to help you identify and develop your God-given spiritual Gifts. Read each statement and on the answer sheet that is included, rate on a scale from 0-4 How that statement is true in your life today. This will take awhile because there are 96 questions. Take your time. **(This survey is used by permission from the website http://www.oaklandumc.com)**

1. I enjoy working behind the scenes, taking care of little details.
2. I usually step forward and assume leadership in a group where none exists.
3. When in a group I tend to recognize and approach those who are sitting or stand- ing alone.
4. I have the ability to recognize a need, and to get the job done, no matter how trivial the task.
5. I have the ability to organize ideas, people and projects to reach a specific goal.
6. People often say I have good spiritual judgment.
7. I am very confident of achieving great things for the glory of God.
8. I am asked to sing or play a musical instrument at church functions.
9. God has used me to communicate the gospel in a language unknown to me.
10. Through my prayers God has made the impossible possible.
11. I have an ability to use my hands in a creative way to design and build things.
12. I have seen my prayers heal people.
13. I enjoy giving money to those in serious financial need.
14. I enjoy ministering to people in hospitals, prisons, or rest homes to comfort them.
15. I often have insights that offer practical solutions to difficult problems.
16. I have understood issues or problems in the church and seen answers when
    Others didn't.
17. I enjoy encouraging and giving counsel to those who are discouraged.
18. I have an ability to thoroughly study a passage of scripture, and then share it with others.
19. I presently have the responsibility for the spiritual growth of one or more young Christians.
20. Other people respect me as an authority in spiritual matters.
21. I have an ability to learn foreign languages.
22. God often reveals to me the direction He desires the body of Christ to move in.
23. I enjoy spending time with non-Christians, especially with hopes of telling them about Jesus.
24. Whenever I hear reports on the news or in conversation about needy situations, I am burdened
    To pray.
25. I would like to assist the pastors or other leaders so they will have more time to
    Accomplish their essential and priority ministries.
26. I don't mind asking others to accomplish an important ministry for the church.
27. I enjoy entertaining guests and making them feel "at home" when they visit.
28. I enjoy serving others, no matter how simple or little the task.

29. I am a very organized person who sets goals and makes plans to reach them.

30. I am a good judge of character, and can spot a spiritual phony.

31. I often step out and start projects that other people won't attempt, and the pro-jects
    Are usually successful.

32. I believe I could sing well in the choir.

33. Praying in tongues is personally meaningful to me in my prayer life.

34. God has used me to make things happen which were far beyond human means.

35. I enjoy doing things like woodworking, crocheting, sewing, metal work, stained glass, etc.

36. I enjoy praying for those who are physically and emotionally ill, for God to heal them.

37. I joyfully give money to the church well above my tithe.

38. I feel compassion for people who are hurting and lonely, and like to spend con- siderable
    Time with them to cheer them up.

39. God has enabled me to choose correctly between several complex options in
    An important decision, when no one else knew what to do.

40. I enjoy studying difficult questions about God's Word, and I am able to find more answers
    Easily and more quickly than others.

41. People often tell me their problems, and I encourage them.

42. When a question arises from a difficult Bible passage, I am motivated to re- search the answer.

43. I like to give of my own free time to meet other's needs.

44. I would be willing and excited to start a new church.

45. I can adapt easily to culture, language, and lifestyle, other than my own, and would like to
    Use my adaptability to minister in foreign countries.

46. I will always speak up for Christian principle & even when what I say isn't popular
    And people think I'm narrow-minded or hardheaded.

47. I find it easy to invite a person to accept Jesus as their Savior.

48. I believe prayer is the most important thing a Christian can do.

49. I enjoy relieving others of routine tasks so they can get special projects done.

50. I can guide and manage a group of people toward achieving a specific goal.

51. I enjoy meeting new people and introducing them to others in the group.

52. I am very dependable for getting things done on time, and I don't need much praise and thanks

53. I easily delegate significant responsibilities to other people.

54. I am able to distinguish between right and wrong in complex spiritual matters that other
    People can't seem to figure out.

55. I trust in God's faithfulness for a bright future, even when everything looks bad.

56. I enjoy singing, and people say I have a good voice.

57. I have been overwhelmed by the Holy Spirit during prayer or worship, and be- gan
    To speak in tongues.

58. God has blessed my prayers so that supernatural results have come from other- wise Impossible situations.

59. I find satisfaction in meeting people's need by making something for them.

60. God regularly speaks to me concerning people's illnesses, so that I can pray For them.

61. I wouldn't mind lowering my standard of living to give more to the church, And others in need.

62. I want to do whatever I can for the needy people around me, even if I have to give up something.

63. People often seek my advice when they don't know what to do.

64. I have an ability to gather information from several sources to discover the an- swer to A question, or learn more about a subject.

65. I feel a need to challenge others to better themselves, especially in their spiritual Growth, without condemning them.

66. Others listen and enjoy my teaching of the scriptures.

67. I enjoy working with people, and desire to help them be the best person they can for the Lord.

68. I am accepted as a spiritual authority in other parts of the country or the world.

69. I would like to present the gospel in a foreign language, in a country whose culture And lifestyle is different than my own.

70. I feel a need to speak God's messages from the Bible so people will know what God Expects of them.

71. I would like to tell others how to become a Christian, and give them the invita- tion To receive Jesus in their life.

72. Many of my prayers for others have been answered by the Lord.

73. I enjoy helping others get their work done, and don't need a lot of public recognition.

74. People respect my opinion and follow my direction.

75. I would like to use my home to get acquainted with newcomers and visitors to the church.

76. I enjoy helping people in any type of need, and feel a sense of satisfaction in meeting that need.

77. I am comfortable making important decisions, even under pressure.

78. People come to me for help in distinguishing between spiritual truth and error.

79. I often exercise my faith through prayer, and God answers my prayers in excit- ing ways.

80. I believe the Lord could use me in the choir to deliver a message through song.

81. I have spoken in a language unknown to me, that when interpreted brought a blessing to Those who heard.

82. God uses me to work miracles for the glory of His kingdom.

83. People say I am gifted with my hands.

84. People often seek me out to pray for their physical healing.

85. When I give money to someone, I don't expect anything in return, and Often give anonymously.

86. When I hear of people without jobs who can't pay their bills, I do what I can to help them.

87. God enables me to make appropriate application of biblical truth to practical situations.

88. I can recognize difficult biblical truths and principles on my own, and I enjoy this.

89. People will tell me things they won't tell anyone else, and say I am easy To talk to.

90. I am organized in my thinking and systematic in my approach to presenting Bible lessons to a group of people.

91. I help Christians who have wandered away from the Lord find their way back to A growing relationship with Him.

92. I would be excited to share the gospel and form new groups of Christians in areas where There aren't many churches.

93. I have no racial prejudice, and have a sincere appreciation for people very Different from myself.

94. I find it relatively easy to apply biblical promises to present day situations.

95. I have a strong desire to help non-Christians find salvation through Jesus Christ.

96. Prayer is my favorite ministry in the church, and I spend a great deal of time on it.

# SPIRITUAL GIFTS DISCOVERY
# ANSWER SHEET

### Select the value from 0 – 4 that the statement is
### True in your life.

0 – Not at all

1 – Little

2 – Moderately

3 – Considerably

4 – Strongly

Name_____

| ANSWERS | | | | TOTAL | ROW | GIFT |
|---|---|---|---|---|---|---|
| 1. | 25. | 49. | 73. | | A | |
| 2. | 26. | 50. | 74. | | B | |
| 3. | 27. | 51. | 75. | | C | |
| 4. | 28. | 52. | 76. | | D | |
| 5. | 29. | 53. | 77. | | E | |
| 6. | 30. | 54. | 78. | | F | |
| 7. | 31. | 55. | 79. | | G | |
| 8. | 32. | 56. | 80. | | H | |
| 9. | 33. | 57. | 81. | | I | |
| 10. | 34. | 58. | 82. | | J | |
| 11. | 35. | 59. | 83. | | K | |
| 12. | 36. | 60. | 84. | | L | |
| 13. | 37. | 61. | 85. | | M | |
| 14. | 38. | 62. | 86. | | N | |
| 15. | 39. | 63. | 87. | | O | |
| 16. | 40. | 64. | 88. | | P | |
| 17. | 41. | 65. | 89. | | Q | |
| 18. | 42. | 66. | 90. | | R | |
| 19. | 43. | 67. | 91. | | S | |
| 20. | 44. | 68. | 92. | | T | |
| 21. | 45. | 69. | 93. | | U | |
| 22. | 46. | 70. | 94. | | V | |
| 23. | 47. | 71. | 95. | | W | |
| 24. | 48. | 72. | 96. | | X | |

**After answering the 96 questions, complete the Total column, and identify top three gifts
By referring to the Gifts Key on the following page.**

**My top three Spiritual Gifts are:** 1. _____

2. _____

3. _____

# GIFTS KEY

A. HELPS

B. LEADERSHIP

C. HOSPITALITY

D. SERVICE

E. ADMINISTRATION

F. DISCERNMENT

G. FAITH

H. MUSIC

I. LANGUAGES (TONGUES)

J. MIRACLES

K. CRAFTSMANSHIP

L. HEALING

M. GIVING

N. MERCY

O. WISDOM

P. KNOWLEDGE

Q. EXHORTATION

R. TEACHING

S. PASTOR/SHEPHERD

T. APOSTLESHIP

U. MISSIONARY

V. PROPHECY

W. EVANGELISM

X. INTERCESSION

# The New Covenant

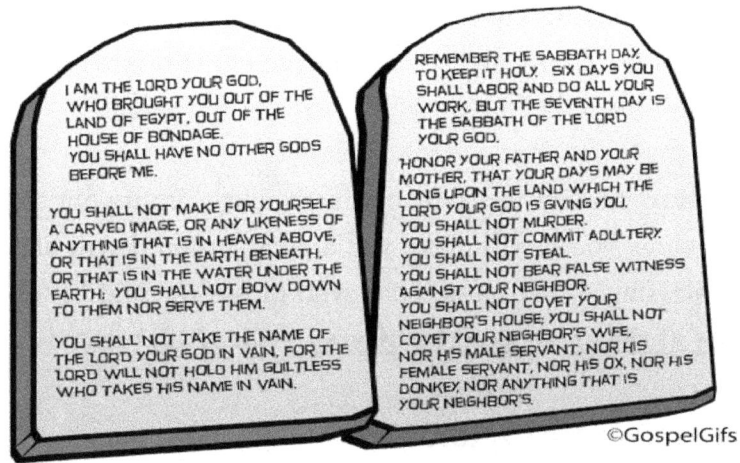

I AM THE LORD YOUR GOD, WHO BROUGHT YOU OUT OF THE LAND OF EGYPT, OUT OF THE HOUSE OF BONDAGE. YOU SHALL HAVE NO OTHER GODS BEFORE ME.

YOU SHALL NOT MAKE FOR YOURSELF A CARVED IMAGE, OR ANY LIKENESS OF ANYTHING THAT IS IN HEAVEN ABOVE, OR THAT IS IN THE EARTH BENEATH, OR THAT IS IN THE WATER UNDER THE EARTH; YOU SHALL NOT BOW DOWN TO THEM NOR SERVE THEM.

YOU SHALL NOT TAKE THE NAME OF THE LORD YOUR GOD IN VAIN, FOR THE LORD WILL NOT HOLD HIM GUILTLESS WHO TAKES HIS NAME IN VAIN.

REMEMBER THE SABBATH DAY, TO KEEP IT HOLY. SIX DAYS YOU SHALL LABOR AND DO ALL YOUR WORK, BUT THE SEVENTH DAY IS THE SABBATH OF THE LORD YOUR GOD.

HONOR YOUR FATHER AND YOUR MOTHER, THAT YOUR DAYS MAY BE LONG UPON THE LAND WHICH THE LORD YOUR GOD IS GIVING YOU.
YOU SHALL NOT MURDER.
YOU SHALL NOT COMMIT ADULTERY.
YOU SHALL NOT STEAL.
YOU SHALL NOT BEAR FALSE WITNESS AGAINST YOUR NEIGHBOR.
YOU SHALL NOT COVET YOUR NEIGHBOR'S HOUSE; YOU SHALL NOT COVET YOUR NEIGHBOR'S WIFE, NOR HIS MALE SERVANT, NOR HIS FEMALE SERVANT, NOR HIS OX, NOR HIS DONKEY, NOR ANYTHING THAT IS YOUR NEIGHBOR'S.

©GospelGifs

**Now therefore, our God, the great, the mighty, and awesome God, who keeps covenant and mercy..." (Nehemiah 9:32)**

In the Old Testament, God made covenants with mankind. A covenant is an agreement. It is a contract between God and man that God initiates. It is always God who initiates the covenant and it can also be understood as a promise. A perfect example is when God made a covenant with Noah to not ever destroy the earth by flood. Let's read:

## God's Covenant With Noah

[11] Thus I establish My covenant with you: Never again shall all flesh be cut off by the waters of the flood; never again shall there be a flood to destroy the earth."

[12] And God said: "**This is the sign of the covenant** which I make between Me and you, and every living creature that is with you, for perpetual generations: [13] I set My rainbow in the cloud, and it shall be for the sign of the covenant between Me and the earth. [14] It shall be, when I bring a cloud over the earth, that the rainbow shall be seen in the cloud; [15] and I will remember My covenant which *is* between Me and you and every living creature of all flesh; the waters shall never again become a flood to destroy all flesh. [16] The rainbow shall be in the cloud, and I will look on it to remember the everlasting covenant between God and every living creature of all flesh that *is* on the earth." [17] And God said to Noah, "This *is* the sign of the covenant which I have established between Me and all flesh that *is* on the earth." **(Genesis 9:11-17)(NKJV)**

God also made covenant's with Abraham and Moses These covenants were agreements made between them. If you broke the agreement you had also broken the covenant with God, and would be cut off from the Grace of God. When God made covenants, the agreements and promises would also follow the descendants. God would bless the family and the families after. This is what God told Abraham. Let's read the text:

"Now the Lord had said to Abram: Get out of your country, from your family and from your father's house, to a land that I will show you. I will make you a great nation; I will bless you and make your name great; and you shall be a blessing. I will bless those who bless you, and I will curse him who curses you; **and in you all the families of the earth shall be blessed**." **(Gen. 12:1-3)**

## God also changes Abram's name to Abraham:

[5] What's more, I am changing your name. It will no longer be Abram. Instead, you will be called Abraham, for you will be the father of many nations. [6] I will make you extremely fruitful. Your descendants will become many nations, and kings will be among them!

[7] "I will confirm my covenant with you and your descendants after you, from generation to generation. This is the everlasting covenant: I will always be your God and the God of your descendants after you. [8] And I will give the entire land of Canaan, where you now live as a foreigner, to you and your descendants. It will be their possession forever, and I will be their God." **(Genesis 17:5-10) (NLT)**

Our loving God fulfills every promise He ever made. We need to always remember God's promises. We need to think for a moment about what God has already done for us and be grateful for what He has given us (Jesus Christ). Nothing else matters, not anything that goes wrong, because God's promises are much greater than our problems. A great example is when Jacob's decedents, who became slaves in Egypt, cried out. God came because of the covenant (Promise) that was made with Abraham and when he died the covenant followed Isaac and Jacob, so that when Jacob's decedents became slaves and began to cry out to God, He remembered his promise. Let's read:

"...the Israelites groaned in their slavery and cried out, and their cry for help because of their slavery went up to God. God heard their groaning and **He remembered His covenant with Abraham, with Isaac and with Jacob**. So God looked on the Israelites and was concerned about them."**(Ex.2: 23-25 NIV)**

And God spoke to Moses and said to him: "I am the LORD. I appeared to Abraham, to Isaac, and to Jacob, as God Almighty, but by My name LORD I was not known to them. I have also established My covenant with them, to give them the land of Canaan, the land of their pilgrimage, in which they were strangers. And I have also heard the groaning of the children of Israel whom the Egyptians keep in bondage, and I have remembered My covenant.

Therefore say to the children of Israel: 'I am the LORD; I will bring you out from under the burdens of the Egyptians, I will rescue you from their bondage, and I will redeem you with an outstretched arm and with great judgments. I will take you as My people, and I will be your God. Then you shall know that I am the LORD your God who brings you out from under the burdens of the Egyptians. And I will bring you into the land which I swore to give to Abraham, Isaac, and Jacob; and I will give it to you as a heritage: I am the LORD.'" **(Ex. 6:2-8)**

God kept his promise and had Moses and his brother Aaron go and help lead the people out of Egypt. They took the Israelites out of slavery, freeing them from the hand of Pharaoh, because He had made a previous covenant. Just like when we receive Jesus Christ as our Lord and Savior, and become doers of his word (not just hearers) we become recipients of the outcome of God's promises. When you trust in God and become more obedient to God's instructions, the showering of promises fall on you, and you will begin to experience and see that life becomes easier and much more fulfilling.

Even when the drama comes the promises of God will come. Our hurdles and struggles will not impact us as hard as they once did because we do not live in an old mind set of depending on 'self,' but depend on God to help us in our time of need. We live by faith and hunger more for God's provision, and when we call out to the Lord we become saved in every area of our life, because we trust in God. He will come to those who believe in Him. He said just be patient and have faith.

God Is not a man, so he does not lie. He Is not human, so he does not change his mind.
Has he ever spoken and failed to act? Has he ever promised and not carried it through?
**Number 23:19 (NLT)**

Abraham was obedient. He trusted God with all he had, even with his son. He was willing to give his son as a sacrifice but God did not permit Abraham to go through with it. God knew Abraham trusted Him because God knew Abraham's heart, and that he would have sacrificed his son for Him. Through the actions of Abraham we see that God comes first. Abraham loved God more than his family. Just think, if you were willing to sacrifice your son without reservation! This is an act of total faith and a deeper understanding of who God is. Walking in total faith, to me, is true love for God. Have total faith in your Creator! The covenant through God and Abraham was held and unbreakable, and followed even after Abraham's death, through his decedents.

God forgave Aaron and the Israelites when they broke their covenant with God. God had answered the prayer of the Israelites to help get them out of slavery. God had spoken to the Israelites through Moses. He gave them commandments and instructions to follow to separate them as His people, and the Israelites agreed to everything, including not worshiping other Gods. God says He is a jealous God and we are not to worship any other Gods.  Let's read the text:

"For you shall worship no other god, for the LORD, whose name is Jealous, is a jealous God" **(Exodus 34:14)** "You shall make no molded gods for yourselves. **(Exodus 34:17) (NKJV)**

After the agreement was made and the Israelites continued to follow God they complained and murmured about not having the types of food they used to eat, and how they had eaten well in Egypt. They wanted to eat meat instead of the manna, so God provided meat as well as shelter, and everything that was needed. One day God called Moses to meet with him. When Moses was gone longer than expected the Israelites got impatient and complained to Aaron about not knowing where Moses was. They decided they wanted a new God to lead them, after they had agreed not to follow any other Gods! Let's read the text:

**The Gold Calf**

32 When the people saw how long it was taking Moses to come back down the mountain, they gathered around Aaron. "Come on," they said, "make us some gods who can lead us. We don't know what happened to this fellow Moses, who brought us here from the land of Egypt."

[2] So Aaron said, "Take the gold rings from the ears of your wives and sons and daughters, and bring them to me."[3] All the people took the gold rings from their ears and brought them to Aaron. [4] Then Aaron took the gold, melted it down, and molded it into the shape of a calf. When the people saw it, they exclaimed, "O Israel, these are the gods who brought you out of the land of Egypt!"

[5] Aaron saw how excited the people were, so he built an altar in front of the calf. Then he announced, "Tomorrow will be a festival to the LORD!"

When they decided to worship a Golden Calf they did not think about how God had answered their prayers and parted the sea to get them out of slavery, or the meat that was given daily as they had requested. God's love for them and His miracles were not good enough the minute Moses was gone too long. Instead of remembering all the things God had done and how great God was for answering their cries, they turned their back on God and said we need a new God. They went back to old traditions. Even today when God does not move fast enough a lot of us go back to a slave mindset, and decide to live a displeasing lifestyle for temporal pleasures. We find it hard to hold onto our agreement, our promise of change that we spoke to God about in our heart. If we were under the old covenant we could not have a relationship with God.

So even though our love fails time and time again, God's love never fails. He made a promise and despite the Israelites breaking their covenant with God, and despite God being angry with the Israelites and displeased with their behavior, He forgave them in order to fulfill His promise that was made to Abraham. Let's read the text:

**God mad** [7] The LORD told Moses, "Quick! Go down the mountain! Your people, whom you brought from the land of Egypt have corrupted themselves. [8] How quickly they have turned away from the way I commanded them to live! They have melted down gold and made a calf, and they have bowed down and sacrificed to it. They are saying, 'These are your gods, O Israel, who brought you out of the land of Egypt.'"

[9] Then the LORD said, "I have seen how stubborn and rebellious these people are. [10] **Now leave me alone so my fierce anger can blaze against them, and I will destroy them**. Then I will make you, Moses, into a great nation." [11] But Moses tried to pacify the LORD his God. "O LORD!" he said. "Why are you so angry with your own people whom you brought from the land of Egypt with such great power and such a strong hand? [12] Why let the Egyptians say, 'Their God rescued them with the evil intention of slaughtering them in the mountains and wiping them from the face of the earth'? Turn away from your fierce anger. Change your mind about this terrible disaster you have threatened against your people! [13] **Remember your servants Abraham, Isaac, and Jacob. You bound yourself with an oath to them, saying, 'I will make your descendants as numerous as the stars of heaven. And I will give them all of this land that I have promised to your descendants, and they will possess it forever.'"**

[14] **So the LORD changed his mind about the terrible disaster he had threatened to bring on his people. (Exodus 32:7-14) (NLT)**

God decided not to destroy them because He had made an agreement; a covenant with Abraham. God is so merciful that He continues to love us, even though we continue to fall short in some of the same ways as the Israelites did by becoming ungrateful, complaining, and worshiping other Gods. We quickly forget that He gave his only begotten son for us when we desire to put others things in our lives before God. It is obvious through our actions when we have turned our backs on God. When things do not go our way, instead of spending time with God by talking about our situations and circumstances we quickly go to 'self' and to other people, places, and things that can never fulfill us as God can.

Now because of the love of God who gave his only begotten son, Jesus Christ, our Lord and Savior, we are not under the old covenant anymore, which would have been too hard for any human being to keep. Having faith in God and believing in the finished works of Jesus Christ gives us eternal life. Jesus is the perfect sacrifice, and believing in Him by faith gives us a relationship with God. The new covenant is through the blood of Jesus Christ, sacrificed on the cross and risen on the third day. The promises of Abraham belong to anyone who believes in Jesus Christ, our Lord and Savior. Let's read the text:

He has enabled us to be ministers of his new covenant. This is a covenant not written laws, but of the Spirit. The old written covenant ends in death; but under the new covenant, the Spirit gives life. **(2 Corinthians 3:6) (NLT)**

[20] After supper he took another cup of wine and said, "This cup is the new covenant between God and his people—an agreement confirmed with my blood, which is poured out as a sacrifice for you. **(Luke 22:20) (NLT)**

[11] He came to his own people, and even they rejected him. [12] But to all who believed him and accepted him, he gave the right to become children of God. **(John 1:12) (NLT)**

## Faith in Jesus Extended Abraham's Blessing to the believer.

[29] And now that you belong to Christ, you are the true children of Abraham. You are his heirs, and God's promise to Abraham belongs to you.   **(Galatians 3:29) (NLT)**

In the same way, "Abraham believed God, and God counted him as righteous because of his faith." The real children of Abraham, then, are those who put their faith in God. What's more, the Scriptures looked forward to this time when God would declare the Gentiles to be righteous because of their faith. God proclaimed this good news to Abraham long ago when he said, "All nations will be blessed through you." **(Galatians 3:6-8) (NLT)**

So as believers we are blessed by God regardless of our circumstances or lack of health, wealth, etc. If you are lacking in these areas it may be because you are lacking in faith, and or have not made good lifestyle choices, but let's be honest. We can do all the right things and we can still have health problems, etc. Rain falls on the just and the unjust. Going through struggles does not mean we are not blessed. Troubles prove that the devil stays busy, and we are not of this world so we see the unfairness, the greed, and the evil schemes of the devil and his demons. It is their job to continue to pressure God's people into believing there is no God. So as believers we have to stand in faith. We all will get through this life and complete our purpose when we keep our eyes on God, and not on our circumstances. Never give up and always keep the faith.

When we believe in Jesus and the reason Jesus had to die for our sins, and that only God can satisfy the Law requirements of a perfect life, and perfect sacrifice that cleanses us of our sins, we not only become children of God but we also become children of Abraham. All believers in Jesus, whether Jew or Gentile became Abraham's spiritual descendants. Praise God for the fulfillment of the promise.

## A New Covenant

## Christ's Sacrifice Once for All

10 The old system under the Law of Moses was only a shadow, a dim preview of the good things to come, not the good things themselves. The sacrifices under that system were repeated again and again, year after year, but they were never able to provide perfect cleansing for those who came to worship. [2] If they could have provided perfect cleansing, the sacrifices would have stopped, for the worshipers would have been purified once for all time, and their feelings of guilt would have disappeared.

[3] But instead, those sacrifices actually reminded them of their sins year after year. [4] For it is not possible for the blood of bulls and goats to take away sins. [5] That is why, when Christ came into the world, he said to God,

"You did not want animal sacrifices or sin offerings.
  But you have given me a body to offer.
[6] You were not pleased with burnt offerings
  Or other offerings for sin.
[7] Then I said, 'Look, I have come to do your will, O God—
  As is written about me in the Scriptures.'"

[8] First, Christ said, "You did not want animal sacrifices or sin offerings or burnt offerings or other offerings for sin, nor were you pleased with them" (though they are required by the law of Moses). [9] Then he said, "Look, I have come to do your will." **He cancels the first covenant in order to put the second into effect.** [10] For God's will was for us to be made holy by the sacrifice of the body of Jesus Christ, once for all time. [11] Under the old covenant, the priest stands and ministers before the altar day after day, offering the same sacrifices again and again, which can never take away sins. [12] But our High Priest offered himself to God as a single sacrifice for sins, good for all time. **Then he sat down in the place of honor at God's right hand. [13] There he waits until his enemies are humbled and made a footstool under his feet. [14] For by that one offering he forever made perfect those who are being made holy.**

[15] And the Holy Spirit also testifies that this is so. For he says,

[16] "This is the new covenant I will make
  with my people on that day, says the LORD:
I will put my laws in their hearts,
  And I will write them on their minds."

[17] Then he says, "I will never again remember their sins and lawless deeds."[18] And when sins have been forgiven, there is no need to offer any more sacrifices. **(Hebrews 10)**

But now Jesus, our High Priest, has been given a ministry that is far superior to the old priesthood, for he is the one who mediates for us a far better covenant with God, based on better promises. **(Hebrews 8:6) (NLT)**

This is why we come in Jesus name. Jesus mediates for all of us to have a relationship with God. God is our Father and Creator. No need to worship anyone or anything outside of Jesus Christ, because nothing dead can give eternal life. As a believer I know the truth. I believe in the finished works of Jesus Christ. When I put my faith in the world, and the people in it, I was lost and spiritually dead. I was miserable and unhappy. Nothing ever worked out for me until I put my faith in God and made a decision to change my old way of thinking. I then let God orchestrate everything in my life to help me get through and God still continues to do that for me to this day.

When I surrendered and realized the lies I had been living, I repented and got baptized. I came to God in spirit and in truth. He guided me and this is when I witnessed and experienced being filled with the Holy Spirit. No one was around me at that time when this happened. I was alone in prayer and talking to God and I asked God to be with me. I admitted to myself and God that I was not only a mess but also a sinner, and I asked for God to help me. I have to be honest in that I have found everything God says and what is written in the Bible to be completely true. You have to go to God and trust in God. Do not worry what your friends and family are doing. No one can save you but God. I experienced the old way and now being a new creation in Christ Jesus, my death sentence is no longer.

[8] God saved you by his grace when you believed. And you can't take credit for this; it is a gift from God. [9] Salvation is not a reward for the good things we have done, so none of us can boast about it. [10] For we are God's masterpiece. He has created us anew in Christ Jesus, so we can do the good things he planned for us long ago. **(Ephesians 2:8-10) (NLT)**

Glory Hallelujah!
Jesus
Set Me Free

# Sabotage & Self Sabotage

The danger of sabotage is that it is something that is done intentionally. You can work hard on something because you once believed in what you were doing and then, all of a sudden, you find yourself in a place of panic, fear, and insecurity, feeling inadequate. Suddenly, you say to yourself, "I can't do it." This sometimes happens right around the time when a person is at the finish line of a project or goal, or in the beginning of starting something new. And there is no logical or rational explanation for why you can't do the things that you want to do or why you cannot have the things that you want to have. You will find yourself downplaying the importance of a task or idea when before you were passionate about it. Satan is big on sabotaging people. God says in John 10:10, "The thief's purpose is to steal and kill and destroy." God is telling us that in anything and everything we attempt to do in this lifetime, we will have challenges, and you can best believe one of the biggest challenges is sabotage.

Satan loves to steal your dreams and kill your desires and destroy God's people. He will do it through your friends, family, and co-workers as well. Just stop and think about what is going on around you right now. You can clearly see the sabotage, but we get so busy and emotionally tired that we are unable to recognize Satan's devices in our daily lives. We seem to find ourselves not being able to finish or attempt to start what God wants us to do due to circumstances. We start to direct all our passion and focus on the drama and forget about what we once loved. I remember when this happened to me; it was the hardest thing I had to swallow, realizing that by my actions I turned away from God by looking for happiness in the material world.

I got totally away from doing ministry and praying and looking to serve. I chose to do the opposite and focused on worldly things. Not long after, I lost my house, business, and finances. My business associates were thieves; they were stealing contracts. The store I opened was soon closed. I lost my good-standing credit, all because I got so caught up in the material world. I became lost and consumed in it. When it was all over, I lost everything and was full of debt. I remember thinking back and asking myself, *how did I even get here?* I was doing so well, spending time praying to God, always taking the opportunity to serve, and God was being glorified in my life. As soon as my business grew, I grew and I increased but God decreased. I stopped my fellowship with God and had no time for church. I quickly forgot about God; I was too busy seeking more and more stuff. I found myself alone and broke.

I remember the fear of being homeless and tears pouring down my face as I was sitting alone. I remember the devil saying, "Where's your God now?" as if God left me when it was the other way around. The devil likes us to blame God for everything. He manipulates us and lies to us and then, when we are stuck, he twists scripture and makes you feel like, "Oh, but you're a believer and all this is happening to you! So, maybe there is no God." He throws up a huge blinking neon-colored sign, "Where is your God?" The Holy Spirit showed me quickly how I chose to chase money and money had begun to be my God and I was getting the curse of what chasing material things gets you, so when the devil asked me, "Where is God?" I thought about his question at that moment and I knew where God was—WITH ME! I had to choose what relationship I was going to have in the future: one with God or one with Satan. And I said out loud, "Look, devil! You can have this house; I am sticking with the Lord in good and in bad. I do not care. I believe God is with me." And God was. After that I stood on faith in God, despite my financial struggles and wrong choices. God had come to my rescue once again. I had wasted a lot of time and money, but God knew I trusted him despite my bad decisions. God got me into a more affordable home which I loved more than the one I had, and it was bought with someone else's money. Remember, I did not have any money to put down on a new house.

My business did not completely die. God showed me a better and an easier way in which I benefitted from my business without working as hard. God is a God of restoration, so it is important that no matter what your battle is to stay on the playing field by asking God for help. Don't quit! Just think of it as being on a football team and you're running with the ball, the ball being your dream, and you're going to the finish line when here come several huge burdens, or obstacles. Satan is trying to trip you so you drop the ball (your dream). Give the burdens to God. Pray to God and tell God what Satan is doing. Satan likes to make our burdens heavy and impossible to carry.

Then Jesus said, "Come to me, all of you who are weary and carry heavy burdens, and I will give you rest. [29] Take my yoke upon you. Let me teach you, because I am humble and gentle at heart, and you will find rest for your souls. [30] For my yoke is easy to bear, and the burden I give you is light." **(Mathew 11: 28-30)**

God is saying, "Let me deal with the problems that Satan brings by having faith in me. I am much stronger than anyone and anything and you cannot fight Satan, but I can. If you pass the obstacles and burdens to me, you can keep running straight ahead toward the finish line. Whether you make it or the ball drops, you win because you have the number one player on your team— God! So regardless if things do not work out as you planned, it does not mean you quit and get angry and hang up your dreams. Instead, take a time-out to go and put on all of God's armor so that you will be able to stand firm against all the strategies of the devil. The devil's strategy is to make you believe you cannot do the things you can do. And if you believe that you can and attempt to try by walking in faith, the devil will start throwing arrows at you from all directions. Then, the devil starts to remind you of all the horrible things that you have done in the past and the bad and embarrassing things that others have done to you,

So you start to feel like a failure rather than victorious. The shame and guilt come in and we start to self-sabotage because the devil, Satan, was given a doorway into our thought process. This is his way of making people feel as though God is not with us, so we abort greatness and make excuses for why we cannot get passed our struggles and in the end, we do it to ourselves because we allow Satan to discredit us rather than let God strengthen us.

I have seen some people, not all, go through school and get their degree, but instead of working in their field, they suddenly feel they need to go back to school rather than take a leap into their field while taking a class, because Satan put fear into their thought process and they suddenly feel inadequate and not good enough. They start to believe they could not actually perform well in that profession or they start to feel it was not what they really wanted, so they go another direction because Satan told them that. People can be confused and can abort the original plan and become frustrated; then, years down the road, they have a bunch of degrees but never made an impact because they prematurely aborted all dreams due to Satan comes in the door they left open. Due to fear, doubt, or anger, they never get through the door. They stand at the door because of the unknown and are afraid. Every time they get close to going through the door, Satan sabotages their mindset. This is why God said to change the way you think. Don't get caught up in the past or in negative thoughts. God says, "For as a man thinks in his heart, so is he."

In **2 Tim 1:7** it is written: "For God has not given us a spirit of fear, but of power and of love and of a sound mind."

It is so important to be around people who will encourage you and will pray for you and help you during your struggles. Don't waste your time with people who only want to complain and never try to do anything differently. They quickly throw in the towel or make excuses why they can't get passed the door. It will only bring you down, and if things are not working for them, and they always seem to be in a negative frame of mind, then they will keep you at the door as well. We need to walk ahead, and as soon as you get passed the door, and the minute the haters come talking about what you cannot do, close the door and find new friends who understand your journey and have faith, because the ones that do not are in your life to do nothing more than pull you back with them. It is time to break out and walk into what God has always had for you.

Satan told me to stop writing this book you are reading right now. He says to me, "Angel, you do not know what you're talking about." Satan told me no one will read this book. And the whole time that I have been writing this book I experienced the unexpected. I have been laid off during the time I am writing this book. I have had computer crashes and lost material. I have had negative thoughts about the content I am writing. I started to second guess myself  because Satan reminds me that I am not good with punctuation and that I have so much more to learn about the Bible, so who do I think I am too

Actually write a workbook to help anyone? Satan knows I have addiction issues, especially with food. I find myself frustrated over all of Satan's arrows that he throws at my mind as I am writing, and I find myself wanting to stop typing this book and go and eat because then I can comfort myself with food—another lie from Satan.

Praise be to God for his "Holy Spirit" that dwells in me and counsels me. God says, "Angel, stay focused and do not fall for the enemy's tricks. Don't give up and stay in prayer and fellowship with me and your Christian family. Pray and watch!" God tells me, "Angel, I have people who will proofread your book. I have given them a gift; they will help you." God says, "Angel, you know enough to know that people overcome by the blood of the lamb, who is Jesus, and by the word of your testimony keep sharing the truth, the word of God, and Satan will flee. And when he comes back, because Satan always does, remind him that you are a child of God and it is not you who does the good work but it is God!"

The devil put it in Judas' heart to betray Jesus. **Luke 22:3, John 13:2**
Satan filled Ananias' heart to lie to the Holy Spirit about his gift. **Acts 5:3**

Satan will try and sabotage every area of your life if you let him; scriptures prove it. He will throw every arrow that he can find to break you and stop your dreams from coming true. And if you believe what Satan says, he then has your heart and you will self-sabotage. It is never too late. I had good intentions and I believed Satan's lies that materials would make me happy, so I dropped the ball and Satan took the ball, my dream, and tried to run with it. Satan probably thought this was it for me. But he forgot Psalms 34:17-19, "The righteous cry out, and the LORD hears them; he delivers them from all their troubles. 18 The LORD is close to the brokenhearted and saves those who are crushed in spirit. 19 A righteous man may have many troubles, but the LORD delivers him from them all."

Satan fumbled the ball, my dreams, but the Lord picked them all up and gave them all back to me!
21 And it shall come to pass, that whosoever shall call on the name of the Lord shall be saved.
   **(Acts 2:21)**

**JUST CALL ON THE NAME OF THE LORD!**

# THE "KNOTS" PRAYER

*Dear God,*

*Please untie the knots*
*that are in my mind,*
*My heart and my life.*

*Remove the have nots,*
*the can nots*
*and the do nots*
*That I have*
*In my mind.*

*Erase the will nots,*
*may nots,*
*And might nots*
*That find a home*
*In my heart.*

*Release me from*
*the could nots,*
*would nots*
*and should nots*
*That obstructs my life.*

*And most of all, dear God…*

*I ask that you*
*Remove from my mind,*
*My heart and my life…*

*all of the am nots*
*That I am allowing*
*To hold me back,*
*Especially the thought*
*That I am not good enough.*
**I ask these things in Jesus name Amen**

*~ Anonymous*

141

The thief's purpose is to steal and kill and destroy. My purpose is to give them a rich and satisfying life.  **(John 10:10) (NLT)**

No one shall separate the hearts joined by God

a threefold cord is not quickly broken
Ecclesiastes 4:12

### Sabotage & Self Sabotage

**Assignment:** Now that we know Satan the devil is here to steal, kill, and destroy. Think about what dreams and goals have you had that were sabotaged. Journal your thoughts.

**Action:** Sabotage always distorts the truth and God's purpose is to give us a rich and satisfying life. So write down a list of goals that you will accomplish now by standing on faith and the word of God. Pray for God to get you back on the right path God wants you to be successful! Journal your thoughts.

1)_____

2)_____

3)_____

4)_____

5)_____

Journaling your thoughts and feelings helps you process events and release emotions. Journaling is a great tool for problem solving. Throughout this workbook you will find pages to journal your thoughts and dreams, and to document prayer requests and testimonials.

## JOURNAL

*Write down your thoughts and share them with the group.*

Date: _____

_____

_____

_____

_____

_____

_____

_____

_____

_____

_____

_____

_____

_____

_____

_____

_____

_____

_____

_____

> For God speaks again and again, though people do not recognize it. He speaks in dreams, in visions of the night, when deep sleep falls on people as they lie in their beds. He whispers in their ears and terrifies them with warnings. He makes them turn from doing wrong; he keeps them from pride. He protects them from the grave, from crossing over the river of death. **(Job 33:14-18) (NLT)**

# DREAM JOURNAL

Day: _____              Date: _____

Bedtime: _____           Time Awake: _____

**Dream Details:**

_____

_____

_____

_____

_____

_____

_____

**Significance or Symbolism:**

_____

_____

_____

_____

_____

# Why Did God Let Them Die?

## THE ACT OF SATAN

We all have lost someone we loved and some of us are having a difficult time moving on because we feel that the one that we loved so much was taken away from us prematurely—so young, so suddenly, so drastically. We're devastated, so we ask why did God let them die. I, too, have lost someone I miss very much, my younger brother Kirk. It took me a long time to recover from his death. I did not understand why someone so sweet and beautiful had to suffer a mental illness and then die so young. I still miss my brother, but I know I will see him again because I am a born-again Christian and so is my brother. And when you are a child of God, regardless of when or how you die, God promises you eternal life, which means you do not die; you are just absent from your body here on earth while your spirit is present with God. Let's read two texts that confirm this:

*Jesus told her, "I am the resurrection and the life. Anyone who believes in me will live, even after dying. 26 Everyone who lives in me and believes in me will never ever die." (John 11:25-26) (NLT)*

### The Temporal and Eternal

5 For we know that when this tent we live in—our body here on earth—is torn down, God will have a house in heaven for us to live in, a home he himself has made, which will last forever. 2 And now we sigh, so great is our desire that our home which comes from heaven should be put on over us; 3 by being clothed with it we shall not be without a body. 4 While we live in this earthly tent, we groan with a feeling of oppression; it is not that we want to get rid of our earthly body, but that we want to have the heavenly one put on over us, so that what is mortal will be transformed by life. 5 God is the one who has prepared us for this change, and he gave us his Spirit as the guarantee of all that he has in store for us. 6 So we are always full of courage. We know that as long as we are at home in the body we are away from the Lord's home. 7 For our life is a matter of faith, not of sight. 8 We are full of courage and would much prefer to leave our home in the body and be at home with the Lord. **(2 Corinthians 5:1-8) (GNT)**

We know one day we all have to die from this body, but our spirit will live when we choose to be born again. In the meantime, we are all on borrowed time and God, as we can see in the text, waits for us to be with him when our time comes. However, Satan, the devil, who is our enemy, wants to kill us before our time. Let's read the text:

[8] Be sober, be vigilant; because your adversary the devil, as a roaring lion, walketh about, seeking whom he may devour: **(1 Peter 5:8) (KJV)**

God says to be sober and yet we see many of God's people hooked on drugs because Satan brought the drugs in to tempt God's people into becoming addicted. Satan has caused people so much pain and frustration that people have committed suicide. This is why we must be alert, and the best way is to know the truth and the only way to know the truth is by reading the word of God, the Bible, for yourself, so Satan can no longer deceive you so easily. God has told us that we are hurting ourselves by our own free will. Let's read the text:

6 My people are destroyed for lack of knowledge: because thou hast rejected knowledge, I will also reject thee, that thou shalt be no priest to me: seeing thou hast forgotten the law of thy God, I will also forget thy children. **(Hosea 4:6) (KJV)**

When we choose not to believe God and when we choose a life outside of the will of God, then whom are we serving? Let's read the text:

You are from your father the devil, and you choose to do your father's desires. He was a murderer from the beginning and does not stand in the truth, because there is no truth in him. When he lies, he speaks according to his own nature, for he is a liar and the father of lies. *(John 8:44) (NRSV)*

So, if God warned us of the act of Satan the devil, why are we ignoring the obvious, especially in today's world with all the killings, murders, kidnappings, bombs, terrorist attacks, drug busts, etc.? God loves us. He said, "The thief does not come except to steal, and to kill, and to destroy. I have come that they may have life, and that they may have it more abundantly." *(John 10:10) (NKJV)*

God does not want his people to die. That is why he gave his only begotten son Jesus. "For God so loved the world, that he gave his only Son, that whoever believes in him should not perish but have eternal life." *(John 3:16)*

God made it clear to us who is doing the killing—Satan! We all have free will and people are using their free will to do evil. They have turned away from God and are serving Satan, and Satan sets up traps all day every day, and God said to watch and be alert! The devil has set up accidents and deceives people into believing that certain lifestyle choices will be okay, and the next thing you know, someone has been killed or has killed another. This is the act of Satan and his demons. Satan killed all of Job's kids in the book of *Job*. Let's read the text:

Your sons and your daughters were eating and drinking wine in their eldest brother's house, 19 And behold, there came a great [whirlwind] from the desert, and smote the four corners of the house, and it fell upon the young people and they are dead, and I alone have escaped to tell you. 20 Then Job arose and tore his robe and shaved his head and fell down upon the ground and worshiped21 And said, Naked
(without possessions) came I [into this world] from my mother's womb, and naked

(Without possessions) shall I depart. The Lord gave and the Lord has taken away; blessed (praised and magnified in worship) be the name of the Lord! 22 In all this Job sinned not nor charged God foolishly. *(Job 1:18-22) (AMP)*

We also have to stop pointing the finger at God and be more like Job, to love God even in our trials, and to praise God in good and bad. Because when we trust in God like Job did, God will restore us in every area. When Job trusted in God despite his wife and friends' negativity, Job prayed and never blamed God. God totally restored Job and he will do the same for us. Let's read the text:

So the Lord blessed Job in the second half of his life even more than in the beginning. For now he had 14,000 sheep, 6,000 camels, 1,000 teams of oxen, and 1,000 female donkeys. 13 He also gave Job seven more sons and three more daughters. 14 He named his first daughter Jemimah, the second Keziah, and the third Keren-happuch.

God always restores what has been taken from the ones whom he loves. Satan, on the other hand, likes tragedies and to constantly cause deaths so people will be hurt and in pain and so consumed that they cannot see the love of God or get any help. But we learn the truth about God and understand that the kingdom of God cannot be destroyed, and that born-again Christians live forever with God because we believe in Jesus and we know it is he who fights for us. Jesus knows the acts of Satan and this is why he has warned us to "Go into all the world and preach the Good News to everyone. 16 Anyone who believes and is baptized will be saved. But anyone who refuses to believe will be condemned." *(Mark 16:15-18) (NLT)*

The reason why people will be condemned is because they are living in Satan's world, which will only lead to death, until you repent of your sins and receive Jesus Christ as your only Lord and Savior in confession and baptism, then you are being saved from this fallen world. If you choose not to, who then can save you? Satan cannot save anyone. It is not in his nature. Let's read the text of the true nature of Satan:

He was a murderer from the beginning and does not stand in the truth, because there is no truth in him. When he lies, he speaks according to his own nature, for he is a liar and the father of lies. **(John 8:44)**

See, Satan does not want anyone to be saved; he wants us dead. Satan does not want to lose any followers. He is a spirit opposite from God. Satan wants to tempt people into using their free will for evil. And this is why you see all these tragedies and deaths. It is all by the act of Satan. So why is it that when things go wrong we blame God? One of the biggest reasons is that Satan has tricked people into believing that he is nothing more than a figure of one's imagination. People even dress up at Halloween as the devil because they feel it is harmless and cute like a cartoon character. Satan likes to trick our mind into thinking he is nothing more than a fluffy kitty cat, but God said, "Stay alert! Watch out for your great enemy, the devil, he prowls around like a roaring lion, looking for someone to devour." **(1 Peter 5:8)**

God warns us that when by our free will and choices we do not believe God, then we make a choice to believe Satan, the devil. And what Satan desires, his only desire and focus, is to steal, kill, and destroy God's people. Some of us have turned away from the Bible, yet when we read the text in 2 Timothy 3:16, it tells us what the Bible is really for. Let's read:

*All Scripture is inspired by God and is useful to teach us what is true and to make us realize what is wrong in our lives. It corrects us when we are wrong and teaches us to do what is right.* **(2 Timothy 3:16)**

So how would we know what is true and what is wrong in our lives if we do not read the Bible? Let's read the text :

In the beginning was the Word, and the Word was with God, and the Word was God. He was in the beginning with God. All things were made through Him, and without Him nothing was made that was made. In Him was life, and the life was the light of men. And the light shines in the darkness, and the darkness did not comprehend it. *(John 1 NKJV)*

When we hear the word of God and read our Bible, we are in God's presence. He speaks to us through his word and we learn about Jesus and how he was always with God from the beginning. Only through Jesus will we be saved, so if we are too consumed with our jobs or spending time playing video games, watching TV, clubbing, doing everything else but understanding the word of God and getting to know the truth—that he gave his only son Jesus and we can only be saved through Jesus, then Satan has you right where he wants you, lacking knowledge. Then, you begin to hate God and love the world (Satan). That is why God says to change the way you think, renew your mind. How we think is where we live. God has come for us to move us out of this world into the kingdom of heaven with him. Let's read the text:

"Let not your hearts be troubled. Believe in God; believe also in me. In my Father's house are many rooms. If it were not so, would I have told you that I go to prepare a place for you? And if I go and prepare a place for you, I will come again and will take you to myself, that where I am you may be also. And you know the way to where I am going." *(John 14:1-2)*

Now it is time to examine and take a look at which direction your life is going and start making the necessary adjustments. Starting over is what God intended us to do from the beginning when he gave his only begotten son Jesus Christ. God is love and he forgives us when we go to him and repent and turn away from sin and show love for our one and only true God, by following his commands and believing what he says and also knowing the truth about the acts of Satan and his demons, and the true character of God.

²² But the fruit of the Spirit is love, joy, peace, long-suffering, kindness, goodness, faithfulness, ²³ gentleness, self-control. Against such there is no law. **(Galatians 5:22-23) (NKV)**

## Free Will

Don't blame the Lord for your sin; the Lord does not cause what he hates. Don't claim that he has misled you; he doesn't need the help of sinners to accomplish his purposes. The Lord hates evil in all its forms, and those who fear the Lord find nothing attractive in evil. When, in the beginning, the Lord created human beings, he left them free to do as they wished. If you want to, you can keep the Lord's commands. You can decide whether you will be loyal to him or not. He has placed fire and water before you; reach out and take whichever you want. You have a choice between life and death; you will get whichever you choose. The Lord's wisdom and power are great, and he sees everything. He is aware of everything a person does, and he takes care of those who fear him. He has never commanded anyone to be wicked or given anyone permission to sin.

**Joshua 24:15** - And if it seem evil unto you to serve the LORD, choose you this day whom ye will serve; whether the gods which your fathers served that [were] on the other side of the flood, or the gods of the Amorites, in whose land ye dwell: but as for me and my house, we will serve the LORD!

## Can the dead really live again?

²⁸ Don't be so surprised! Indeed, the time is coming when all the dead in their graves will hear the voice of God's Son, ²⁹ and they will rise again. Those who have done good will rise to experience eternal life, and those who have continued in evil will rise to experience judgment. **( John 5:28-29) (NLT)**

THEN I SAW A NEW HEAVEN AND A NEW EARTH, FOR THE FIRST HEAVEN AND THE FIRST EARTH HAD PASSED AWAY, AND THE SEA WAS NO MORE. AND I SAW THE HOLY CITY, NEW JERUSALEM, COMING DOWN OUT OF HEAVEN FROM GOD, PREPARED AS A BRIDE ADORNED FOR HER HUSBAND. AND I HEARD A LOUD VOICE FROM THE THRONE SAYING, "BEHOLD, THE DWELLING PLACE OF GOD IS WITH MAN. HE WILL DWELL WITH THEM, AND THEY WILL BE HIS PEOPLE, AND GOD HIMSELF WILL BE WITH THEM AS THEIR GOD. HE WILL WIPE AWAY EVERY TEAR FROM THEIR EYES, AND DEATH SHALL BE NO MORE, NEITHER SHALL THERE BE MOURNING, NO MORE CRYING, NOR PAIN ANYMORE, FOR THE FORMER THINGS HAVE PASSED AWAY." **(REVELATION 21:1-4)**

*"But if you are careful to obey him, following all my instructions,*
*Then I will be an enemy to your enemies,*
*And I will oppose those who oppose you."*
(Exodus 23:22) (NLT)

O Lord, my God,
You are my safe place
in all the storms of life

## Why Did God Let Them Die?

### THE ACT OF SATAN

**Assignment:** Trusting in God can be very difficult when we do not know the word of God, so how can we allow God to give us a revelation or a better understanding of the love that God truly has for us. Discuss what is stopping you from reading the word of God and obeying God.

**Action:** Now that you know God protects those who will listen and follow all his instructions what changes do you need to make to surrender to God's will. Write down what distractions are taking your focus and time away from reading the word of God. A good place to start reading in the bible is in the New Testament.

1)_____

2)_____

3)_____

4)_____

5)_____

Journaling your thoughts and feelings helps you process events and release emotions. Journaling is a great tool for problem solving. Throughout this workbook you will find pages to journal your thoughts and dreams, and to document prayer requests and testimonials.

## JOURNAL

*Write down your thoughts and share them with the group.*

Date: _____

_____

_____

_____

_____

_____

_____

_____

_____

_____

_____

_____

_____

_____

_____

_____

_____

_____

_____

_____

For God speaks again and again, though people do not recognize it. He speaks in dreams, in visions of the night, when deep sleep falls on people as they lie in their beds. He whispers in their ears and terrifies them with warnings. He makes them turn from doing wrong; he keeps them from pride. He protects them from the grave, from crossing over the river of death. **(Job 33:14-18) (NLT)**

# DREAM JOURNAL

Day: _____          Date: _____

Bedtime: _____          Time Awake: _____

**Dream Details:**

_____

_____

_____

_____

_____

_____

_____

**Significance or Symbolism:**

_____

_____

_____

_____

_____

# Scriptures For Healing

God has done miraculous healing through the work of Jesus Christ and through faith in God. Today is no different. There have been thousands and thousands who have witnessed people become totally healed when chances for healing were slim. When asked how they were healed, they admitted it was God who answered their prayers. When we stay in continued prayer and believe that God is the healer, we will see the miracle healing of God in our lives. God is not a onetime healer. If he has done it for one he will do it for another. It is God's will for us to be healed. We must stand on the word of God and ask not only for healing but Divine Healing. I have witnessed God's Divine Healing and you can too. Here are some scriptures that will encourage and help focus on healing, both spiritually and physically.

LORD, help!" they cried in their trouble, and he saved them from their distress. [20] He sent out his word and healed them, snatching them from the door of death. **(Psalms 107:19-20) (NLT)**

[24] Who his own self bare our sins in his own body on the tree, that we, being dead to sins, should live unto righteousness: by whose stripes ye were healed. **(1 Peter 2:24) (KJV)**

[25] And ye shall serve the LORD your God, and he shall bless thy bread, and thy water; and I will take sickness away from the midst of thee. **(Exodus 23:25)**

[26] He said, "If you will listen carefully to the voice of the LORD your God and do what is right in his sight, obeying his commands and keeping all his decrees, then I will not make you suffer any of the diseases I sent on the Egyptians; for I am the LORD who heals you." **(Exodus 15:16) (NLT)**

My son, give attention to my words; Incline your ear to my sayings. Do not let them depart from your eyes; Keep them in the midst of your heart. For they are life to those who find them, And health to all their flesh. **(Prov 4:20-22 NKJV)**

Beloved, I wish above all things that thou mayest prosper and be in health, even as thy soul prospereth. **(3 John 1:2 KJV)**

"And these signs will follow those who believe: In My name they will cast out demons; they will speak with new tongues; "they will take up serpents; and if they drink anything deadly, it will by no means hurt them; they will lay hands on the sick, and they will recover." **(Mark 16:17-18 NKJV)**

Is anyone among you sick? Let him call for the elders of the church, and let them pray over him, anointing him with oil in the name of the Lord. And the prayer of faith will save the sick, and the Lord will raise him up. And if he has committed sins, he will be forgiven. **(James 5:14-15 NKJV)**

And behold, a leper came and worshipped Him, saying, "Lord, if You are willing, You can make me clean. Then Jesus put out His hand and touched him, saying, "I am willing; be cleansed." Immediately his leprosy was cleansed. **(Mat 8:2-3 NKJV)**

"Therefore I say to you, whatever things you ask when you pray, believe that you receive them, and you will have them. **(Mark 11:24 NKJV)**

For all the promises of God in Him are Yes, and in Him Amen, to the glory of God through us.
**(2 Cor 1:20 NKJV)**

Now this is the confidence that we have in Him, that if we ask anything according to His will, He hears us. And if we know that He hears us, whatever we ask, we know that we have the petitions that we have asked of Him. **(1 John 5:14-15 NKJV)**

But if the Spirit of Him who raised Jesus from the dead dwells in you, He who raised Christ from the dead will also give life to your mortal bodies through His Spirit who dwells in you. **(Rom 8:11 NKJV)**

He heals the brokenhearted and bandages their wounds. **(Psalms 147:3) (NLT)**

They that wait upon the LORD shall renew their strength; they shall mount up with wings as eagles; they shall run, and not be weary; and they shall walk, and not faint. — Isaiah 40:31

# Give your life to Christ

*°. ℘ ★. ℘°℘°•。 ☆☆ *°. ℘ ★.℘°℘℘ ★°℘℘ ★.℘°℘☆ *°. ℘ ★.℘°℘°•。 ☆☆

This book and study have taught us the true love of God. God is for us and has never been against us. He is the only one who truly loves us unconditionally. No one can help us but God and God has always planned from the beginning to be that key person in our life to show us the right path to take in this Journey that we call life.

When we get honest with ourselves and we let go of the toxic things in our life and start to move forward and build a loving relationship with God, He will create something better and something greater than you can ever imagine. God already has a plan for all of us. When you know that Jesus is the Son of God nothing can stop you once you stand on the word of God!

## Prayer

If you've never given your life to Jesus, I invite you to pray this simple prayer from your heart:

*Dear God, I know I'm a sinner and I need a Savior. I believe You sent Your only Son, Jesus, to die on the cross for me, to pay the price for my sins, and that He rose again. Come into my life and make me new. I receive You as my Lord and Savior in Jesus name. Amen!*

## Congratulations!

When you become a follower of Jesus heaven celebrates and rejoices with you!

"In the same way, there is joy in the presence of God's angels when even one sinner repents." **(Luke 15:10 (NLT)**

[20] My old self has been crucified with Christ. It is no longer I who live, but Christ lives in me. So I live in this earthly body by trusting in the Son of God, who loved me and gave himself for me. **(Galatians 2:20)**

If you declare with your mouth, "Jesus is Lord," and believe in your heart that God raised him from the dead, you will be saved. **(Romans 10:9) (NLT)**

# A Prayer For Protection And Strength

☆ *° .℘ ★.℘°℘°•。 ☆☆ *° .℘ ★.℘°℘℘ ★°℘℘ ★.℘°℘☆ *° .℘ ★.℘°℘°•。 ☆☆

## Psalm 91

Those who live in the shelter of the Most High will find rest in the shadow of the Almighty. This I declare about the LORD:

He alone is my refuge, my place of safety; he is my God, and I trust him. For he will rescue you from every trap and protect you from deadly disease. He will cover you with his feathers. He will shelter you with his wings. His faithful promises are your armor and protection. Do not be afraid of the terrors of the night, nor the arrow that flies in the day. Do not dread the disease that stalks in darkness, nor the disaster that strikes at midday.

Though a thousand fall at your side, though ten thousand are dying around you, these evils will not touch you. Just open your eyes, and see how the wicked are punished. If you make the LORD your refuge, if you make the Most High your shelter, no evil will conquer you; no plague will come near your home. For he will order his angels to protect you wherever you go. They will hold you up with their hands so you won't even hurt your foot on a stone. You will trample upon lions and cobras; you will crush fierce lions and serpents under your feet!

The LORD says, "I will rescue those who love me. I will protect those who trust in my name. When they call on me, I will answer; I will be with them in trouble. I will rescue and honor them. I will reward them with a long life and give them my salvation."

# Faith as small as a mustard seed

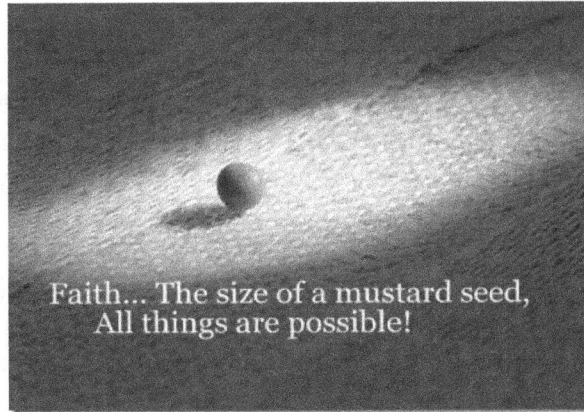

Faith... The size of a mustard seed,
All things are possible!

Mustard seeds are small and round like in the picture we see above. The seeds are usually about 1 or 2 mm in diameter. In the *New Testament*, the mustard seed is used by Jesus in a parable as a model for the kingdom of God in that it initially starts small but grows to be the biggest of all garden plants. Faith is also spoken about in the context of a mustard seed. Now let's read the text in **Luke 17:5-11;** this is a conversation between Jesus and His apostles about their faith:

The apostles said to the Lord, "Show us how to increase our faith." The Lord answered, "If you had faith **even as small as a mustard seed**, you could say to this mulberry tree, 'May you be uprooted and thrown into the sea,' and it would obey you!" **(Luke 17:5-11)**

First, we read that the apostles are asking Jesus how to increase their faith. This was an ongoing struggle with the apostles because even though they saw Jesus feed over 5,000 people with a few loaves of bread and two fish, bring people back from the dead, stop the wind and the waves when they were on a boat in a life-threatening storm, and do all kinds of miracles that no one else in the entire world could do, they still struggled with their faith. They still asked, "SHOW US how to increase our faith." But God said that faith comes by HEARING! Let's read what God said about having faith:

[17] So faith comes from hearing, that is, hearing the Good News about Christ. **(Romans 10:17) (NLT)**

Faith is the confidence that what we hope for will actually happen; it gives us assurance about things we cannot see. **(Hebrews 11:1) (NLT)**

Jesus showed the apostles' faith all day long for 3 years, but did they believe? You will always struggle in your faith if you do not put your trust and faith in what God can do THROUGH YOU! And the way to increase your faith is to believe that the things which are impossible with men are possible with God! When you truly believe and have faith in God, you will put it into action by speaking and obeying God. In the beginning the apostles struggled with putting what was taught by God into action because of their lack of faith. Let's read some scriptures for examples of little faith:

## Little Faith

*Matthew 14:29-31* He said, "Come." So Peter got out of the boat and walked on the water and came to Jesus. But when he saw the wind, he was afraid, and beginning to sink he cried out, "Lord, save me." Jesus immediately reached out his hand and took hold of him, saying to him, "O you of little faith, why did you doubt?"

*Luke 12:27-28* "Consider the lilies, how they grow: they neither toil nor spin, yet I tell you, even Solomon in all his glory was not arrayed like one of these. But if God so clothes the grass, which is alive in the field today, and tomorrow is thrown into the oven, how much more will he clothe you, O you of little faith!" (Jesus speaking)

*Matthew 8:26* And he said to them, "Why are you afraid, O you of little faith?" Then he rose and rebuked the winds and the sea, and there was a great calm. (Jesus speaking to His Apostles)

*Matthew 17:20* He said to them, "Because of your little faith. For truly, I say to you, if you have faith like a grain of mustard seed, you will say to this mountain, 'Move from here to there,' and it will move, and nothing will be impossible for you." (Jesus Speaking)

Because of our little faith, Jesus is saying, "YOU DON'T TRUST ME!" Wow! This is hard to swallow when you know you love God, but our actions show we can be faithless in Him. So the disciples are asking, "SHOW US how to increase our faith." God is saying, "Don't just go through the motions; step out in faith and know who I am, so you can truly believe and finish the race.

We see in the scriptures above that the apostles had little faith because of doubt, unbelief, and fear. They wanted to do what God asked, but they were looking to themselves to accomplish it rather than letting go and letting God work it out.

## Let's read the text that reminds us that God works it out for us *and not to take our eyes off Jesus*:

We do this by keeping our eyes on Jesus, the champion who initiates and perfects our faith. Because of the joy awaiting him, he endured the cross, disregarding its shame. Now he is seated in the place of honor beside God's throne. *(Hebrews 12:2) (NLT)*

Let's read what God says in **Matthew 17:20:**

"Because of your little faith. For truly, I say to you, if you have faith like a grain of mustard seed, you will say to this mountain, 'Move from here to there,' and it will move, and nothing will be impossible for you." (Jesus Speaking)

We all know that when you plant and water a seed, it will grow. Now, what happens if you plant a seed and never water it? How would it grow? The disciples are saying, "Show us how to increase our faith," so God is saying that if you want to build your faith, it needs to start small like a mustard seed, because you need to grow in knowing the truth.

Remember, Jesus spent 3 years with the disciples. Why 3 years? Jesus taught them from seed form. He watered the disciples with the word of God. The disciples knew nothing at first. They started small and by following Jesus they were able to learn the truth and do great things. Many were saved through the disciples because they grew in faith from seed form. The spiritual seed of faith can only grow by the word of God and knowing that He is the author and finisher; He is the water for our seed, and the more you trust in Him, the more He can pour into you. Then, you will begin to grow in every area of your life. You will see the change and you will know it is only God who has blessed you, and your faith will increase. Look at yourself as a mustard seed. Will you stay in seed form, or will you allow God to pour into you? The disciples allowed God to pour into them daily for 3 years. Even though they struggled with doubt, unbelief, and fear, they showed up and God said that if you come as you are in small form (small beginnings), as a seed, He will make you grow to do great things. God can only increase our faith if we believe in Him. Let's read the text:

And it is impossible to please God without faith. Anyone who wants to come to him must believe that God exists and that he rewards those who sincerely seek him. **(Hebrews 11:6) (NLT)**

Remember, the disciples sincerely sought God for 3 years!

## The Kingdom of Heaven Is Like a Mustard Seed

"The kingdom of heaven is like a grain of mustard seed that a man took and sowed in his field. It is the smallest of all seeds, but when it has grown it is larger than all the garden plants and becomes a tree, so that the birds of the air come and make nests in its branches **(Matthew 13:31-32) (ESV)**

### Parable of the Mustard Seed

[18] Then Jesus said, "What is the Kingdom of God like? How can I illustrate it? [19] It is like a tiny mustard seed that a man planted in a garden; it grows and becomes a tree, and the birds make nests in its branches."

### Parable of the Yeast

[20] He also asked, "What else is the Kingdom of God like? [21] It is like the yeast a woman used in making bread. Even though she put only a little yeast in three measures of flour, it permeated every part of the dough."

As believers, we have to put what we have heard into action. We must perform our given duties without doubt, which means that we must become doers and follow what He has taught us in His word and not be fearful, because all we need is to put our faith and trust in the finished works of Jesus. We only do what we actually believe, so our obedience to the word of God shows our faith. God is the only good ground. In the parable of the mustard seed, He says a man planted it in a garden and it grew to become a tree and the birds made nests in its branches. Read what is written in the book of John:

[5] "Yes, I am the vine; you are the branches. Those who remain in me, and I in them, will produce much fruit. For apart from me you can do nothing." **(John 15:5) (NLT)**

Then, we also read in the parable of the yeast that "even though she put only a little yeast in three measures of flour, it permeated every part of the dough."

God will work in you and through you as long as you believe in God and do what He tells you to do, obeying all the commands He has given. We must be obedient to all God asks and His plan in our life will produce much fruit. Anything apart from God can do nothing, so I am going to close with two things that come to mind about what God wants us to do, which will also increase our faith in God.

## 1) Serving One Another

**Matthew 25:34-40:**

[34] "Then the King will say to those on his right, 'Come, you who are blessed by my Father, inherit the Kingdom prepared for you from the creation of the world. [35] For I was hungry, and you fed me. I was thirsty, and you gave me a drink. I was a stranger, and you invited me into your home. [36] I was naked, and you gave me clothing. I was sick, and you cared for me. I was in prison, and you visited me.'

[37] "Then these righteous ones will reply, 'Lord, when did we ever see you hungry and feed you? Or thirsty and give you something to drink? [38] Or a stranger and show you hospitality? Or naked and give you clothing? [39] When did we ever see you sick or in prison and visit you?'

[40] "And the King will say, 'I tell you the truth, when you did it to one of the least of these my brothers and sisters, you were doing it to me!'

**Mark 10:42-45:**

[42] So Jesus called them together and said, "You know that the rulers in this world lord it over their people, and officials flaunt their authority over those under them. [43] But among you it will be different. Whoever wants to be a leader among you must be your servant, [44] and whoever wants to be first among you must be the slave of everyone else. [45] For even the Son of Man came not to be served but to serve others and to give his life as a ransom for many."

## 2) Loving One Another

**1 John 4:7:**[7] Dear friends, let us continue to love one another, for love comes from God. Anyone who loves is a child of God and knows God.

## More on Love

[11] For this is the message you heard from the beginning: We should love one another. [12] Do not be like Cain, who belonged to the evil one and murdered his brother. And why did he murder him? Because his own actions were evil and his brother's were righteous. [13] Do not be surprised, my brothers and sisters, if the world hates you. [14] We know that we have passed from death to life, because we love each other. Anyone who does not love remains in death. [15] Anyone who hates a brother or sister is a murderer, and you know that no murderer has eternal life residing in him.

[16] This is how we know what love is: Jesus Christ laid down his life for us. And we ought to lay down our lives for our brothers and sisters. [17] If anyone has material possessions and sees a brother or sister in need but has no pity on them, how can the love of God be in that person? [18] Dear children, let us not love with words or speech but with actions and in truth.

[19] This is how we know that we belong to the truth and how we set our hearts at rest in his presence: [20] If our hearts condemn us, we know that God is greater than our hearts, and he knows everything. [21] Dear friends, if our hearts do not condemn us, we have confidence before God [22] and receive from him anything we ask, because we keep his commands and do what pleases him. [23] And this is his command: to believe in the name of his Son, Jesus Christ, and to love one another as he commanded us. [24] The one who keeps God's commands lives in him, and he in them. And this is how we know that he lives in us: We know it by the Spirit he gave us. **1 John 3:11**

## Love Is the Greatest

13 If I could speak all the languages of earth and of angels, but didn't love others, I would only be a noisy gong or a clanging cymbal. [2] If I had the gift of prophecy, and if I understood all of God's secret plans and possessed all knowledge, and if I had such faith that I could move mountains, but didn't love others, I would be nothing. [3] If I gave everything I have to the poor and even sacrificed my body, I could boast about it; but if I didn't love others, I would have gained nothing.

[4] Love is patient and kind. Love is not jealous or boastful or proud [5] or rude. It does not demand its own way. It is not irritable, and it keeps no record of being wronged. [6] It does not rejoice about injustice but rejoices whenever the truth wins out. [7] Love never gives up, never loses faith, is always hopeful, and endures through every circumstance.

[8] Prophecy and speaking in unknown languages and special knowledge will become useless. But love will last forever! [9] Now our knowledge is partial and incomplete, and even the gift of prophecy reveals only part of the whole picture! [10] But when the time of perfection comes, these partial things will become useless.

[11] When I was a child, I spoke and thought and reasoned as a child. But when I grew up, I put away childish things. [12] Now we see things imperfectly, like puzzling reflections in a mirror, but then we will see everything with perfect clarity. All that I know now is partial and incomplete, but then I will know everything completely, just as God now knows me completely. [13] Three things will last forever—faith, hope, and love—and the greatest of these is love. **(1 Corinthians 13)**

# Bible Reading Plan - Read the Bible in a Year

Follow this schedule and read the entire Bible in a year. Start reading the Bible daily. Say a prayer to God before you begin, asking the Holy Spirit to give you wisdom and understanding, share with friends and family what you have learned.

| | | | |
|---|---|---|---|
| Jan 01 Readings | GENESIS 1:1-2:25<br>MATTHEW 1:1-2:12<br>PSALM 1:1-1:6<br>PROVERBS 1:1-1:6 | Jan 11 Readings | GENESIS 24:52-26:16<br>MATTHEW 8:18-34<br>PSALM 10:1-15<br>PROVERBS 3:7-8 |
| Jan 02 Readings | GENESIS 3:1-4:26<br>MATTHEW 2:13-3:6<br>PSALM 2:1-2:12<br>PROVERBS 1:7-1:9 | Jan 12 Readings | GENESIS 26:17-27:46<br>MATTHEW 9:1-17<br>PSALM 10:16-18<br>PROVERBS 3:9-10 |
| Jan 03 Readings | GENESIS 5:1-7:24<br>MATTHEW 3:7-4:11<br>PSALM 3:1-8<br>PROVERBS 1:10-19 | Jan 13 Readings | GENESIS 28:1-29:35<br>MATTHEW 9:18-38<br>PSALM 11:1-7<br>PROVERBS 3:11-12 |
| Jan 04 Readings | GENESIS 8:1-10:32<br>MATTHEW 4:12-25<br>PSALM 4:1-8<br>PROVERBS 1:20-23 | Jan 14 Readings | GENESIS 30:1-31:16<br>MATTHEW 10:1-23<br>PSALM 12:1-8<br>PROVERBS 3:13-15 |
| Jan 05 Readings | GENESIS 11:1-13:4<br>MATTHEW 5:1-26<br>PSALM 5:1-12<br>PROVERBS 1:24-28 | Jan 15 Readings | GENESIS 31:17-32:12<br>MATTHEW 10:24-11:6<br>PSALM 13:1-6<br>PROVERBS 3:16-18 |
| Jan 06 Readings | GENESIS 13:5-15:21<br>MATTHEW 5:27-48<br>PSALM 6:1-10<br>PROVERBS 1:29-33 | Jan 16 Readings | GENESIS 32:13-34:31<br>MATTHEW 11:7-30<br>PSALM 14:1-7<br>PROVERBS 3:19-20 |
| Jan 07 Readings | GENESIS 16:1-18:15<br>MATTHEW 6:1-24<br>PSALM 7:1-17<br>PROVERBS 2:1-5 | Jan 17 Readings | GENESIS 35:1-36:43<br>MATTHEW 12:1-21<br>PSALM 15:1-5<br>PROVERBS 3:21-26 |
| Jan 08 Readings | GENESIS 18:16-19:38<br>MATTHEW 6:25-7:14<br>PSALM 8:1-9<br>PROVERBS 2:6-15 | Jan 18 Readings | GENESIS 37:1-38:30<br>MATTHEW 12:22-45<br>PSALM 16:1-11<br>PROVERBS 3:27-32 |
| Jan 09 Readings | GENESIS 20:1-22:24<br>MATTHEW 7:15-29<br>PSALM 9:1-12<br>PROVERBS 2:16-22 | Jan 19 Readings | GENESIS 39:1-41:16<br>MATTHEW 12:46-13:23<br>PSALM 17:1-15<br>PROVERBS 3:33-35 |
| Jan 10 Readings | GENESIS 23:1-24:51<br>MATTHEW 8:1-17<br>PSALM 9:13-20<br>PROVERBS 3:1-6 | Jan 20 Readings | GENESIS 41:17-42:17<br>MATTHEW 13:24-46<br>PSALM 18:1-15<br>PROVERBS 4:1-6 |

| | |
|---|---|
| Jan 21 Readings | GENESIS 42:18-43:34<br>MATTHEW 13:47-14:12<br>PSALM 18:16-36<br>PROVERBS 4:7-10 |
| Jan 22 Readings | GENESIS 44:1-45:28<br>MATTHEW 14:13-36<br>PSALM 18:37-50<br>PROVERBS 4:11-13 |
| Jan 23 Readings | GENESIS 46:1-47:31<br>MATTHEW 15:1-28<br>PSALM 19:1-14<br>PROVERBS 4:14-19 |
| Jan 24 Readings | GENESIS 48:1-49:33<br>MATTHEW 15:29-16:12<br>PSALM 20:1-9<br>PROVERBS 4:20-27 |
| Jan 25 Readings | GENESIS 50:1-26<br>EXODUS 1:1-2:10<br>MATTHEW 16:13-17:9<br>PSALM 21:1-13<br>PROVERBS 5:1-6 |
| Jan 26 Readings | EXODUS 2:11-3:22<br>MATTHEW 17:10-27<br>PSALM 22:1-18<br>PROVERBS 5:7-14 |
| Jan 27 Readings | EXODUS 4:1-5:21<br>MATTHEW 18:1-20<br>PSALM 22:19-31<br>PROVERBS 5:15-21 |
| Jan 28 Readings | EXODUS 5:22-7:25<br>MATTHEW 18:21-19:12<br>PSALM 23:1-6<br>PROVERBS 5:22-23 |
| Jan 29 Readings | EXODUS 8:1-9:35<br>MATTHEW 19:13-30<br>PSALM 24:1-10<br>PROVERBS 6:1-5 |
| Jan 30 Readings | EXODUS 10:1-12:13<br>MATTHEW 20:1-28<br>PSALM 25:1-15<br>PROVERBS 6:6-11 |
| Jan 31 Readings | EXODUS 12:14-13:16<br>MATTHEW 20:29-21:22<br>PSALM 25:16-22<br>PROVERBS 6:12-15 |

| | |
|---|---|
| Feb 01 Readings | EXODUS 13:17-15:18<br>MATTHEW 21:23-46<br>PSALM 26:1-12<br>PROVERBS 6:16-19 |
| Feb 02 Readings | EXODUS 15:19-17:7<br>MATTHEW 22:1-33<br>PSALM 27:1-6<br>PROVERBS 6:20-26 |
| Feb 03 Readings | EXODUS 17:8-19:15<br>MATTHEW 22:34-23:12<br>PSALM 27:7-14<br>PROVERBS 6:27-35 |
| Feb 04 Readings | EXODUS 19:16-21:21<br>MATTHEW 23:13-39<br>PSALM 28:1-9<br>PROVERBS 7:1-5 |
| Feb 05 Readings | EXODUS 21:22-23:13<br>MATTHEW 24:1-28<br>PSALM 29:1-11<br>PROVERBS 7:6-23 |
| Feb 06 Readings | EXODUS 23:14-25:40<br>MATTHEW 24:29-51<br>PSALM 30:1-12<br>PROVERBS 7:24-27 |
| Feb 07 Readings | EXODUS 26:1-27:21<br>MATTHEW 25:1-30<br>PSALM 31:1-8<br>PROVERBS 8:1-11 |
| Feb 08 Readings | EXODUS 28:1-43<br>MATTHEW 25:31-26:13<br>PSALM 31:9-18<br>PROVERBS 8:12-13 |
| Feb 09 Readings | EXODUS 29:1-30:10<br>MATTHEW 26:14-46<br>PSALM 31:19-24<br>PROVERBS 8:14-26 |
| Feb 10 Readings | EXODUS 30:11-31:18<br>MATTHEW 26:47-68<br>PSALM 32:1-11<br>PROVERBS 8:27-32 |
| Feb 11 Readings | EXODUS 32:1-33:23<br>MATTHEW 26:69-27:14<br>PSALM 33:1-11<br>PROVERBS 8:33-36 |

| Feb 12 Readings | EXODUS 34:1-35:9<br>MATTHEW 27:15-31<br>PSALM 33:12-22<br>PROVERBS 9:1-6 |
|---|---|
| Feb 13 Readings | EXODUS 35:10-36:38<br>MATTHEW 27:32-66<br>PSALM 34:1-10<br>PROVERBS 9:7-8 |
| Feb 14 Readings | EXODUS 37:1-38:31<br>MATTHEW 28:1-20<br>PSALM 34:11-22<br>PROVERBS 9:9-10 |
| Feb 15 Readings | EXODUS 39:1-40:38<br>MARK 1:1-28<br>PSALM 35:1-16<br>PROVERBS 9:11-12 |
| Feb 16 Readings | LEVITICUS 1:1-3:17<br>MARK 1:29-2:12<br>PSALM 35:17-28<br>PROVERBS 9:13-18 |
| Feb 17 Readings | LEVITICUS 4:1-5:19<br>MARK 2:13-3:6<br>PSALM 36:1-12<br>PROVERBS 10:1-2 |
| Feb 18 Readings | LEVITICUS 6:1-7:27<br>MARK 3:7-30<br>PSALM 37:1-11<br>PROVERBS 10:3-4 |
| Feb 19 Readings | LEVITICUS 7:28-9:6<br>MARK 3:31-4:25<br>PSALM 37:12-29<br>PROVERBS 10:5 |
| Feb 20 Readings | LEVITICUS 9:7-10:20<br>MARK 4:26-5:20<br>PSALM 37:30-40<br>PROVERBS 10:6-7 |
| Feb 21 Readings | LEVITICUS 11:1-12:8<br>MARK 5:21-43<br>PSALM 38:1-22<br>PROVERBS 10:8-9 |
| Feb 22 Readings | LEVITICUS 13:1-59<br>MARK 6:1-29<br>PSALM 39:1-13<br>PROVERBS 10:10 |
| Feb 23 Readings | LEVITICUS 14:1-57<br>MARK 6:30-56<br>PSALM 40:1-10<br>PROVERBS 10:11-12 |

| Feb 24 Readings | LEVITICUS 15:1-16:28<br>MARK 7:1-23<br>PSALM 40:11-17<br>PROVERBS 10:13-14 |
|---|---|
| Feb 25 Readings | LEVITICUS 16:29-18:30<br>MARK 7:24-8:10<br>PSALM 41:1-13<br>PROVERBS 10:15-16 |
| Feb 26 Readings | LEVITICUS 19:1-20:21<br>MARK 8:11-38<br>PSALM 42:1-11<br>PROVERBS 10:17 |
| Feb 27 Readings | LEVITICUS 20:22-22:16<br>MARK 9:1-29<br>PSALM 43:1-5<br>PROVERBS 10:18 |
| Feb 28 Readings | LEVITICUS 22:17-23:44<br>MARK 9:30-10:12<br>PSALM 44:1-8<br>PROVERBS 10:19 |
| Mar 01 Readings | LEVITICUS 24:1-25:46<br>MARK 10:13-31<br>PSALM 44:9-26<br>PROVERBS 10:20-21 |
| Mar 02 Readings | LEVITICUS 25:47-27:13<br>MARK 10:32-52<br>PSALM 45:1-17<br>PROVERBS 10:22 |
| Mar 03 Readings | LEVITICUS 27:14-<br>NUMBERS 1:1-54<br>MARK 11:1-26<br>PSALM 46:1-11<br>PROVERBS 10:23 |
| Mar 04 Readings | NUMBERS 2:1-3:51<br>MARK 11:27-12:17<br>PSALM 47:1-9<br>PROVERBS 10:24-25 |
| Mar 05 Readings | NUMBERS 4:1-5:31<br>MARK 12:18-37<br>PSALM 48:1-14<br>PROVERBS 10:26 |
| Mar 06 Readings | NUMBERS 6:1-7:89<br>MARK 12:38-13:13<br>PSALM 49:1-20<br>PROVERBS 10:27-28 |

| | |
|---|---|
| Mar 07 Readings | NUMBERS 8:1-9:23 MARK 13:14-37 PSALM 50:1-23 PROVERBS 10:29-30 |
| Mar 08 Readings | NUMBERS 10:1-11:23 MARK 14:1-21 PSALM 51:1-19 PROVERBS 10:31-32 |
| Mar 09 Readings | NUMBERS 11:24-13:33 MARK 14:22-52 PSALM 52:1-9 PROVERBS 11:1-3 |
| Mar 10 Readings | NUMBERS 14:1-15:16 MARK 14:53-72 PSALM 53:1-6 PROVERBS 11:4 |
| Mar 11 Readings | NUMBERS 15:17-16:40 MARK 15:1-47 PSALM 54:1-7 PROVERBS 11:5-6 |
| Mar 12 Readings | NUMBERS 16:41-18:32 MARK 16:1-20 PSALM 55:1-23 PROVERBS 11:7 |
| Mar 13 Readings | NUMBERS 19:1-20:29 LUKE 1:1-25 PSALM 56:1-13 PROVERBS 11:8 |
| Mar 14 Readings | NUMBERS 21:1-22:20 LUKE 1:26-56 PSALM 57:1-11 PROVERBS 11:9-11 |
| Mar 15 Readings | NUMBERS 22:21-23:30 LUKE 1:57-80 PSALM 58:1-11 PROVERBS 11:12-13 |
| Mar 16 Readings | NUMBERS 24:1-25:18 LUKE 2:1-35 PSALM 59:1-17 PROVERBS 11:14 |
| Mar 17 Readings | NUMBERS 26:1-51 LUKE 2:36-52 PSALM 60:1-12 PROVERBS 11:15 |

| | |
|---|---|
| Mar 18 Readings | NUMBERS 26:52-28:15 LUKE 3:1-22 PSALM 61:1-8 PROVERBS 11:16-17 |
| Mar 19 Readings | NUMBERS 28:16-29:40 LUKE 3:23-38 PSALM 62:1-12 PROVERBS 11:18-19 |
| Mar 20 Readings | NUMBERS 30:1-31:54 LUKE 4:1-30 PSALM 63:1-11 PROVERBS 11:20-21 |
| Mar 21 Readings | NUMBERS 32:1-33:39 LUKE 4:31-5:11 PSALM 64:1-10 PROVERBS 11:22 |
| Mar 22 Readings | NUMBERS 33:40-35:34 LUKE 5:12-28 PSALM 65:1-13 PROVERBS 11:23 |
| Mar 23 Readings | NUMBERS 36:1-13 DEUTERONOMY 1:1-46 LUKE 5:29-6:11 PSALM 66:1-20 PROVERBS 11:24-26 |
| Mar 24 Readings | DEUTERONOMY 2:1-3:29 LUKE 6:12-38 PSALM 67:1-7 PROVERBS 11:27 |
| Mar 25 Readings | DEUTERONOMY 4:1-49 LUKE 6:39-7:10 PSALM 68:1-18 PROVERBS 11:28 |
| Mar 26 Readings | DEUTERONOMY 5:1-6:25 LUKE 7:11-35 PSALM 68:19-35 PROVERBS 11:29-31 |
| Mar 27 Readings | DEUTERONOMY 7:1-8:20 LUKE 7:36-8:3 PSALM 69:1-18 PROVERBS 12:1 |
| Mar 28 Readings | DEUTERONOMY 9:1-10:22 LUKE 8:4-21 PSALM 69:19-36 PROVERBS 12:2-3 |

| | |
|---|---|
| Mar 29 Readings | DEUTERONOMY 11:1-12:32<br>LUKE 8:22-39<br>PSALM 70:1-5<br>PROVERBS 12:4 |
| Mar 30 Readings | DEUTERONOMY 13:1-15:23<br>LUKE 8:40-9:6<br>PSALM 71:1-24<br>PROVERBS 12:5-7 |
| Mar 31 Readings | DEUTERONOMY 16:1-17:20<br>LUKE 9:7-27<br>PSALM 72:1-20<br>PROVERBS 12:8-9 |
| Apr 01 Readings | DEUTERONOMY 18:1-20:20<br>LUKE 9:28-50<br>PSALM 73:1-28<br>PROVERBS 12:10 |
| Apr 02 Readings | DEUTERONOMY 21:1-22:30<br>LUKE 9:51-10:12<br>PSALM 74:1-23<br>PROVERBS 12:11 |
| Apr 03 Readings | DEUTERONOMY 23:1-25:19<br>LUKE 10:13-37<br>PSALM 75:1-10<br>PROVERBS 12:12-14 |
| Apr 04 Readings | DEUTERONOMY 26:1-27:26<br>LUKE 10:38-11:13<br>PSALM 76:1-12<br>PROVERBS 12:15-17 |
| Apr 05 Readings | DEUTERONOMY 28:1-68<br>LUKE 11:14-36<br>PSALM 77:1-20<br>PROVERBS 12:18 |
| Apr 06 Readings | DEUTERONOMY 29:1-30:20<br>LUKE 11:37-12:7<br>PSALM 78:1-31<br>PROVERBS 12:19-20 |
| Apr 07 Readings | DEUTERONOMY 31:1-32:27<br>LUKE 12:8-34<br>PSALM 78:32-55<br>PROVERBS 12:21-23 |

| | |
|---|---|
| Apr 08 Readings | DEUTERONOMY 32:28-52<br>LUKE 12:35-59<br>PSALM 78:56-64<br>PROVERBS 12:24 |
| Apr 09 Readings | DEUTERONOMY 33:1-29<br>LUKE 13:1-21<br>PSALM 78:65-72<br>PROVERBS 12:25 |
| Apr 10 Readings | DEUTERONOMY 34:1-12<br>JOSHUA 1:1-2:24<br>LUKE 13:22-14:6<br>PSALM 79:1-13<br>PROVERBS 12:26 |
| Apr 11 Readings | JOSHUA 3:1-4:24<br>LUKE 14:7-35<br>PSALM 80:1-19<br>PROVERBS 12:27-28 |
| Apr 12 Readings | JOSHUA 5:1-7:15<br>LUKE 15:1-32<br>PSALM 81:1-16<br>PROVERBS 13:1 |
| Apr 13 Readings | JOSHUA 7:16-9:2<br>LUKE 16:1-18<br>PSALM 82:1-8<br>PROVERBS 13:2-3 |
| Apr 14 Readings | JOSHUA 9:3-10:43<br>LUKE 16:19-17:10<br>PSALM 83:1-18<br>PROVERBS 13:4 |
| Apr 15 Readings | JOSHUA 11:1-12:24<br>LUKE 17:11-37<br>PSALM 84:1-12<br>PROVERBS 13:5-6 |
| Apr 16 Readings | JOSHUA 13:1-14:15<br>LUKE 18:1-17<br>PSALM 85:1-13<br>PROVERBS 13:7-8 |
| Apr 17 Readings | JOSHUA 15:1-63<br>LUKE 18:18-43<br>PSALM 86:1-17<br>PROVERBS 13:9-10 |
| Apr 18 Readings | JOSHUA 16:1-18:28<br>LUKE 19:1-27<br>PSALM 87:1-7<br>PROVERBS 13:11 |

| Apr 19 Readings | JOSHUA 19:1-20:9<br>LUKE 19:28-48<br>PSALM 88:1-18<br>PROVERBS 13:12-14 |
|---|---|
| Apr 20 Readings | JOSHUA 21:1-22:20<br>LUKE 20:1-26<br>PSALM 89:1-13<br>PROVERBS 13:15-16 |
| Apr 21 Readings | JOSHUA 22:21-23:16<br>LUKE 20:27-47<br>PSALM 89:14-37<br>PROVERBS 13:17-19 |
| Apr 22 Readings | JOSHUA 24:1-33<br>LUKE 21:1-28<br>PSALM 89:38-52<br>PROVERBS 13:20-23 |
| Apr 23 Readings | JUDGES 1:1-2:9<br>LUKE 21:29-22:13<br>PSALM 90:1-91:16<br>PROVERBS 13:24-25 |
| Apr 24 Readings | JUDGES 2:10-3:31<br>LUKE 22:14-34<br>PSALM 92:1-93:5<br>PROVERBS 14:1-2 |
| Apr 25 Readings | JUDGES 4:1-5:31<br>LUKE 22:35-53<br>PSALM 94:1-23<br>PROVERBS 14:3-4 |
| Apr 26 Readings | JUDGES 6:1-40<br>LUKE 22:54-23:12<br>PSALM 95:1-96:13<br>PROVERBS 14:5-6 |
| Apr 27 Readings | JUDGES 7:1-8:17<br>LUKE 23:13-43<br>PSALM 97:1-98:9<br>PROVERBS 14:7-8 |
| Apr 28 Readings | JUDGES 8:18-9:21<br>LUKE 23:44-24:12<br>PSALM 99:1-9<br>PROVERBS 14:9-10 |
| Apr 29 Readings | JUDGES 9:22-10:18<br>LUKE 24:13-53<br>PSALM 100:1-5<br>PROVERBS 14:11-12 |
| Apr 30 Readings | JUDGES 11:1-12:15<br>JOHN 1:1-28<br>PSALM 101:1-8<br>PROVERBS 14:13-14 |

| May 01 Readings | JUDGES 13:1-14:20<br>JOHN 1:29-51<br>PSALM 102:1-28<br>PROVERBS 14:15-16 |
|---|---|
| May 02 Readings | JUDGES 15:1-16:31<br>JOHN 2:1-25<br>PSALM 103:1-22<br>PROVERBS 14:17-19 |
| May 03 Readings | JUDGES 17:1-18:31<br>JOHN 3:1-21<br>PSALM 104:1-23<br>PROVERBS 14:20-21 |
| May 04 Readings | JUDGES 19:1-20:48<br>JOHN 3:22-4:3<br>PSALM 104:24-35<br>PROVERBS 14:22-24 |
| May 05 Readings | JUDGES 21:1-25<br>RUTH 1:1-22<br>JOHN 4:4-42<br>PSALM 105:1-15<br>PROVERBS 14:25 |
| May 06 Readings | RUTH 2:1-4:22<br>JOHN 4:43-54<br>PSALM 105:16-36<br>PROVERBS 14:26-27 |
| May 07 Readings | 1SAMUEL 1:1-2:21<br>JOHN 5:1-23<br>PSALM 105:37-45<br>PROVERBS 14:28-29 |
| May 08 Readings | 1SAMUEL 2:22-4:22<br>JOHN 5:24-47<br>PSALM 106:1-12<br>PROVERBS 14:30-31 |
| May 09 Readings | 1SAMUEL 5:1-7:17<br>JOHN 6:1-21<br>PSALM 106:13-31<br>PROVERBS 14:32-33 |
| May 10 Readings | 1SAMUEL 8:1-9:27<br>JOHN 6:22-42<br>PSALM 106:32-48<br>PROVERBS 14:34-35 |
| May 11 Readings | 1SAMUEL 10:1-11:15<br>JOHN 6:43-71<br>PSALM 107:1-43<br>PROVERBS 15:1-3 |

| | |
|---|---|
| May 12 Readings | 1SAMUEL 12:1-13:23<br>JOHN 7:1-30<br>PSALM 108:1-13<br>PROVERBS 15:4 |
| May 13 Readings | 1SAMUEL 14:1-52<br>JOHN 7:31-53<br>PSALM 109:1-31<br>PROVERBS 15:5-7 |
| May 14 Readings | 1SAMUEL 15:1-16:23<br>JOHN 8:1-20<br>PSALM 110:1-7<br>PROVERBS 15:8-10 |
| May 15 Readings | 1SAMUEL 17:1-18:4<br>JOHN 8:21-30<br>PSALM 111:1-10<br>PROVERBS 15:11 |
| May 16 Readings | 1SAMUEL 18:5-19:24<br>JOHN 8:31-59<br>PSALM 112:1-10<br>PROVERBS 15:12-14 |
| May 17 Readings | 1SAMUEL 20:1-21:15<br>JOHN 9:1-41<br>PSALM 113:1-114:8<br>PROVERBS 15:15-17 |
| May 18 Readings | 1SAMUEL 22:1-23:29<br>JOHN 10:1-21<br>PSALM 115:1-18<br>PROVERBS 15:18-19 |
| May 19 Readings | 1SAMUEL 24:1-25:44<br>JOHN 10:22-42<br>PSALM 116:1-19<br>PROVERBS 15:20-21 |
| May 20 Readings | 1SAMUEL 26:1-28:25<br>JOHN 11:1-54<br>PSALM 117:1-2<br>PROVERBS 15:22-23 |
| May 21 Readings | 1SAMUEL 29:1-31:13<br>JOHN 11:55-12:19<br>PSALM 118:1-18<br>PROVERBS 15:24-26 |
| May 22 Readings | 2SAMUEL 1:1-2:11<br>JOHN 12:20-50<br>PSALM 118:19-29<br>PROVERBS 15:27-28 |
| May 23 Readings | 2SAMUEL 2:12-3:39<br>JOHN 13:1-30<br>PSALM 119:1-16<br>PROVERBS 15:29-30 |
| May 24 Readings | 2SAMUEL 4:1-6:23<br>JOHN 13:31-14:14<br>PSALM 119:17-32<br>PROVERBS 15:31-32 |
| May 25 Readings | 2SAMUEL 7:1-8:18<br>JOHN 14:15-31<br>PSALM 119:33-48<br>PROVERBS 15:33 |
| May 26 Readings | 2SAMUEL 9:1-11:27<br>JOHN 15:1-27<br>PSALM 119:49-64<br>PROVERBS 16:1-3 |
| May 27 Readings | 2SAMUEL 12:1-31<br>JOHN 16:1-33<br>PSALM 119:65-80<br>PROVERBS 16:4-5 |
| May 28 Readings | 2SAMUEL 13:1-39<br>JOHN 17:1-26<br>PSALM 119:81-96<br>PROVERBS 16:6-7 |
| May 29 Readings | 2SAMUEL 14:1-15:22<br>JOHN 18:1-24<br>PSALM 119:97-112<br>PROVERBS 16:8-9 |
| May 30 Readings | 2SAMUEL 15:23-16:23<br>JOHN 18:25-19:22<br>PSALM 119:113-128<br>PROVERBS 16:10-11 |
| May 31 Readings | 2SAMUEL 17:1-29<br>JOHN 19:23-42<br>PSALM 119:129-152<br>PROVERBS 16:12-13 |
| Jun 01 Readings | 2SAMUEL 18:1-19:10<br>JOHN 20:1-31<br>PSALM 119:153-176<br>PROVERBS 16:14-15 |
| Jun 02 Readings | 2SAMUEL 19:11-20:13<br>JOHN 21:1-25<br>PSALM 120:1-7<br>PROVERBS 16:16-17 |

| | |
|---|---|
| Jun 03 Readings | 2SAMUEL 20:14-21:22<br>ACTS 1:1-26<br>PSALM 121:1-8<br>PROVERBS 16:18 |
| Jun 04 Readings | 2SAMUEL 22:1-23:23<br>ACTS 2:1-47<br>PSALM 122:1-9<br>PROVERBS 16:19-20 |
| Jun 05 Readings | 2SAMUEL 23:24-24:25<br>ACTS 3:1-26<br>PSALM 123:1-4<br>PROVERBS 16:21-23 |
| Jun 06 Readings | 1KINGS 1:1-53<br>ACTS 4:1-37<br>PSALM 124:1-8<br>PROVERBS 16:24 |
| Jun 07 Readings | 1KINGS 2:1-3:2<br>ACTS 5:1-42<br>PSALM 125:1-5<br>PROVERBS 16:25 |
| Jun 08 Readings | 1KINGS 3:3-4:34<br>ACTS 6:1-15<br>PSALM 126:1-6<br>PROVERBS 16:26-27 |
| Jun 09 Readings | 1KINGS 5:1-6:38<br>ACTS 7:1-29<br>PSALM 127:1-5<br>PROVERBS 16:28-30 |
| Jun 10 Readings | 1KINGS 7:1-51<br>ACTS 7:30-50<br>PSALM 128:1-6<br>PROVERBS 16:31-33 |
| Jun 11 Readings | 1KINGS 8:1-66<br>ACTS 7:51-8:13<br>PSALM 129:1-8<br>PROVERBS 17:1 |
| Jun 12 Readings | 1KINGS 9:1-10:29<br>ACTS 8:14-40<br>PSALM 130:1-8<br>PROVERBS 17:2-3 |
| Jun 13 Readings | 1KINGS 11:1-12:19<br>ACTS 9:1-25<br>PSALM 131:1-3<br>PROVERBS 17:4-5 |

| | |
|---|---|
| Jun 14 Readings | 1KINGS 12:20-13:34<br>ACTS 9:26-43<br>PSALM 132:1-18<br>PROVERBS 17:6 |
| Jun 15 Readings | 1KINGS 14:1-15:24<br>ACTS 10:1-23<br>PSALM 133:1-3<br>PROVERBS 17:7-8 |
| Jun 16 Readings | 1KINGS 15:25-17:24<br>ACTS 10:24-48<br>PSALM 134:1-3<br>PROVERBS 17:9-11 |
| Jun 17 Readings | 1KINGS 18:1-46<br>ACTS 11:1-30<br>PSALM 135:1-21<br>PROVERBS 17:12-13 |
| Jun 18 Readings | 1KINGS 19:1-21<br>ACTS 12:1-23<br>PSALM 136:1-26<br>PROVERBS 17:14-15 |
| Jun 19 Readings | 1KINGS 20:1-21:29<br>ACTS 12:24-13:15<br>PSALM 137:1-9<br>PROVERBS 17:16 |
| Jun 20 Readings | 1KINGS 22:1-53<br>ACTS 13:16-41<br>PSALM 138:1-8<br>PROVERBS 17:17-18 |
| Jun 21 Readings | 2KINGS 1:1-2:25<br>ACTS 13:42-14:7<br>PSALM 139:1-24<br>PROVERBS 17:19-21 |
| Jun 22 Readings | 2KINGS 3:1-4:17<br>ACTS 14:8-28<br>PSALM 140:1-13<br>PROVERBS 17:22 |
| Jun 23 Readings | 2KINGS 4:18-5:27<br>ACTS 15:1-35<br>PSALM 141:1-10<br>PROVERBS 17:23 |
| Jun 24 Readings | 2KINGS 6:1-7:20<br>ACTS 15:36-16:15<br>PSALM 142:1-7<br>PROVERBS 17:24-25 |

| | |
|---|---|
| Jun 25 Readings | 2KINGS 8:1-9:13<br>ACTS 16:16-40<br>PSALM 143:1-12<br>PROVERBS 17:26 |
| Jun 26 Readings | 2KINGS 9:14-10:31<br>ACTS 17:1-34<br>PSALM 144:1-15<br>PROVERBS 17:27-28 |
| Jun 27 Readings | 2KINGS 10:32-12:21<br>ACTS 18:1-22<br>PSALM 145:1-21<br>PROVERBS 18:1 |
| Jun 28 Readings | 2KINGS 13:1-14:29<br>ACTS 18:23-19:12<br>PSALM 146:1-10<br>PROVERBS 18:2-3 |
| Jun 29 Readings | 2KINGS 15:1-16:20<br>ACTS 19:13-41<br>PSALM 147:1-20<br>PROVERBS 18:4-5 |
| Jun 30 Readings | 2KINGS 17:1-18:12<br>ACTS 20:1-38<br>PSALM 148:1-14<br>PROVERBS 18:6-7 |
| Jul 01 Readings | 2KINGS 18:13-19:37<br>ACTS 21:1-17<br>PSALM 149:1-9<br>PROVERBS 18:8 |
| Jul 02 Readings | 2KINGS 20:1-22:2<br>ACTS 21:18-36<br>PSALM 150:1-6<br>PROVERBS 18:9-10 |
| Jul 03 Readings | 2KINGS 22:3-23:30<br>ACTS 21:37-22:16<br>PSALM 1:1-6<br>PROVERBS 18:11-12 |
| Jul 04 Readings | 2KINGS 23:31-25:30<br>ACTS 22:17-23:10<br>PSALM 2:1-12<br>PROVERBS 18:13 |
| Jul 05 Readings | 1CHRONICLES 1:1-2:17<br>ACTS 23:11-35<br>PSALM 3:1-8<br>PROVERBS 18:14-15 |
| Jul 06 Readings | 1CHRONICLES 2:18-4:4<br>ACTS 24:1-27<br>PSALM 4:1-8<br>PROVERBS 18:16-18 |
| Jul 07 Readings | 1CHRONICLES 4:5-5:17<br>ACTS 25:1-27<br>PSALM 5:1-12<br>PROVERBS 18:19 |
| Jul 08 Readings | 1CHRONICLES 5:18-6:81<br>ACTS 26:1-32<br>PSALM 6:1-10<br>PROVERBS 18:20-21 |
| Jul 09 Readings | 1CHRONICLES 7:1-8:40<br>ACTS 27:1-20<br>PSALM 7:1-17<br>PROVERBS 18:22 |
| Jul 10 Readings | 1CHRONICLES 9:1-10:14<br>ACTS 27:21-44<br>PSALM 8:1-9<br>PROVERBS 18:23-24 |
| Jul 11 Readings | 1CHRONICLES 11:1-12:18<br>ACTS 28:1-31<br>PSALM 9:1-12<br>PROVERBS 19:1-3 |
| Jul 12 Readings | 1CHRONICLES 12:19-14:17<br>ROMANS 1:1-17<br>PSALM 9:13-20<br>PROVERBS 19:4-5 |
| Jul 13 Readings | 1CHRONICLES 15:1-16:36<br>ROMANS 1:18-32<br>PSALM 10:1-15<br>PROVERBS 19:6-7 |
| Jul 14 Readings | 1CHRONICLES 16:37-18:17<br>ROMANS 2:1-24<br>PSALM 10:16-18<br>PROVERBS 19:8-9 |
| Jul 15 Readings | 1CHRONICLES 19:1-21:30<br>ROMANS 2:25-3:8<br>PSALM 11:1-7<br>PROVERBS 19:10-12 |
| Jul 16 Readings | 1CHRONICLES 22:1-23:32<br>ROMANS 3:9-31<br>PSALM 12:1-8<br>PROVERBS 19:13-14 |

| | |
|---|---|
| Jul 17 Readings | 1CHRONICLES 24:1-26:11<br>ROMANS 4:1-12<br>PSALM 13:1-6<br>PROVERBS 19:15-16 |
| Jul 18 Readings | 1CHRONICLES 26:12-27:34<br>ROMANS 4:13-5:5<br>PSALM 14:1-7<br>PROVERBS 19:17 |
| Jul 19 Readings | 1CHRONICLES 28:1-29:30<br>ROMANS 5:6-21<br>PSALM 15:1-5<br>PROVERBS 19:18-19 |
| Jul 20 Readings | 2CHRONICLES 1:1-3:17<br>ROMANS 6:1-23<br>PSALM 16:1-11<br>PROVERBS 19:20-21 |
| Jul 21 Readings | 2CHRONICLES 4:1-6:11<br>ROMANS 7:1-13<br>PSALM 17:1-15<br>PROVERBS 19:22-23 |
| Jul 22 Readings | 2CHRONICLES 6:12-8:10<br>ROMANS 7:14-8:8<br>PSALM 18:1-15<br>PROVERBS 19:24-25 |
| Jul 23 Readings | 2CHRONICLES 8:11-10:19<br>ROMANS 8:9-25<br>PSALM 18:16-36<br>PROVERBS 19:26 |
| Jul 24 Readings | 2CHRONICLES 11:1-13:22<br>ROMANS 8:26-39<br>PSALM 18:37-50<br>PROVERBS 19:27-29 |
| Jul 25 Readings | 2CHRONICLES 14:1-16:14<br>ROMANS 9:1-24<br>PSALM 19:1-14<br>PROVERBS 20:1 |
| Jul 26 Readings | 2CHRONICLES 17:1-18:34<br>ROMANS 9:25-10:13<br>PSALM 20:1-9<br>PROVERBS 20:2-3 |
| Jul 27 Readings | 2CHRONICLES 19:1-20:37<br>ROMANS 10:14-11:12<br>PSALM 21:1-13<br>PROVERBS 20:4-6 |
| Jul 28 Readings | 2CHRONICLES 21:1-23:21<br>ROMANS 11:13-36<br>PSALM 22:1-18<br>PROVERBS 20:7 |

| | |
|---|---|
| Jul 29 Readings | 2CHRONICLES 24:1-25:28<br>ROMANS 12:1-21<br>PSALM 22:19-31<br>PROVERBS 20:8-10 |
| Jul 30 Readings | 2CHRONICLES 26:1-28:27<br>ROMANS 13:1-14<br>PSALM 23:1-6<br>PROVERBS 20:11 |
| Jul 31 Readings | 2CHRONICLES 29:1-36<br>ROMANS 14:1-23<br>PSALM 24:1-10<br>PROVERBS 20:12 |
| Aug 01 Readings | 2CHRONICLES 30:1-31:21<br>ROMANS 15:1-22<br>PSALM 25:1-15<br>PROVERBS 20:13-15 |
| Aug 02 Readings | 2CHRONICLES 32:1-33:13<br>ROMANS 15:23-16:9<br>PSALM 25:16-22<br>PROVERBS 20:16-18 |
| Aug 03 Readings | 2CHRONICLES 33:14-34:33<br>ROMANS 16:10-27<br>PSALM 26:1-12<br>PROVERBS 20:19 |
| Aug 04 Readings | 2CHRONICLES 35:1-36:23<br>1CORINTHIANS 1:1-17<br>PSALM 27:1-6<br>PROVERBS 20:20-21 |
| Aug 05 Readings | EZRA 1:1-2:70<br>1CORINTHIANS 1:18-2:5<br>PSALM 27:7-14<br>PROVERBS 20:22-23 |
| Aug 06 Readings | EZRA 3:1-4:23<br>1CORINTHIANS 2:6-3:4<br>PSALM 28:1-9<br>PROVERBS 20:24-25 |
| Aug 07 Readings | EZRA 4:24-6:22<br>1CORINTHIANS 3:5-23<br>PSALM 29:1-11<br>PROVERBS 20:26-27 |
| Aug 08 Readings | EZRA 7:1-8:20<br>1CORINTHIANS 4:1-21<br>PSALM 30:1-12<br>PROVERBS 20:28-30 |

| | |
|---|---|
| Aug 09 Readings | EZRA 8:21-9:15<br>1CORINTHIANS 5:1-13<br>PSALM 31:1-8<br>PROVERBS 21:1-2 |
| Aug 10 Readings | EZRA 10:1-44<br>1CORINTHIANS 6:1-20<br>PSALM 31:9-18<br>PROVERBS 21:3 |
| Aug 11 Readings | NEHEMIAH 1:1-3:14<br>1CORINTHIANS 7:1-24<br>PSALM 31:19-24<br>PROVERBS 21:4 |
| Aug 12 Readings | NEHEMIAH 3:15-5:13<br>1CORINTHIANS 7:25-40<br>PSALM 32:1-11<br>PROVERBS 21:5-7 |
| Aug 13 Readings | NEHEMIAH 5:14-7:73<br>1CORINTHIANS 8:1-13<br>PSALM 33:1-11<br>PROVERBS 21:8-10 |
| Aug 14 Readings | NEHEMIAH 7:73-9:21<br>1CORINTHIANS 9:1-18<br>PSALM 33:12-22<br>PROVERBS 21:11-12 |
| Aug 15 Readings | NEHEMIAH 9:22-10:39<br>1CORINTHIANS 9:19-10:13<br>PSALM 34:1-10<br>PROVERBS 21:13 |
| Aug 16 Readings | NEHEMIAH 11:1-12:26<br>1CORINTHIANS 10:14-33<br>PSALM 34:11-22<br>PROVERBS 21:14-16 |
| Aug 17 Readings | NEHEMIAH 12:27-13:31<br>1CORINTHIANS 11:1-16<br>PSALM 35:1-16<br>PROVERBS 21:17-18 |
| Aug 18 Readings | ESTHER 1:1-3:15<br>1CORINTHIANS 11:17-34<br>PSALM 35:17-28<br>PROVERBS 21:19-20 |
| Aug 19 Readings | ESTHER 4:1-7:10<br>1CORINTHIANS 12:1-26<br>PSALM 36:1-12<br>PROVERBS 21:21-22 |
| Aug 20 Readings | ESTHER 8:1-10:3<br>1CORINTHIANS 12:27-13:13<br>PSALM 37:1-11<br>PROVERBS 21:23-24 |
| Aug 21 Readings | JOB 1:1-3:26<br>1CORINTHIANS 14:1-17<br>PSALM 37:12-29<br>PROVERBS 21:25-26 |
| Aug 22 Readings | JOB 4:1-7:21<br>1CORINTHIANS 14:18-40<br>PSALM 37:30-40<br>PROVERBS 21:27 |
| Aug 23 Readings | JOB 8:1-11:20<br>1CORINTHIANS 15:1-28<br>PSALM 38:1-22<br>PROVERBS 21:28-29 |
| Aug 24 Readings | JOB 12:1-15:35<br>1CORINTHIANS 15:29-58<br>PSALM 39:1-13<br>PROVERBS 21:30-31 |
| Aug 25 Readings | JOB 16:1-19:29<br>1CORINTHIANS 16:1-24<br>PSALM 40:1-10<br>PROVERBS 22:1 |
| Aug 26 Readings | JOB 20:1-22:30<br>2CORINTHIANS 1:1-11<br>PSALM 40:11-17<br>PROVERBS 22:2-4 |
| Aug 27 Readings | JOB 23:1-27:23<br>2CORINTHIANS 1:12-2:11<br>PSALM 41:1-13<br>PROVERBS 22:5-6 |
| Aug 28 Readings | JOB 28:1-30:31<br>2CORINTHIANS 2:12-17<br>PSALM 42:1-11<br>PROVERBS 22:7 |
| Aug 29 Readings | JOB 31:1-33:33<br>2CORINTHIANS 3:1-18<br>PSALM 43:1-5<br>PROVERBS 22:8-9 |
| Aug 30 Readings | JOB 34:1-36:33<br>2CORINTHIANS 4:1-12<br>PSALM 44:1-8<br>PROVERBS 22:10-12 |

| Aug 31 Readings | JOB 37:1-39:30<br>2CORINTHIANS 4:13-5:10<br>PSALM 44:9-26<br>PROVERBS 22:13 |
|---|---|
| Sep 01 Readings | JOB 40:1-42:17<br>2CORINTHIANS 5:11-21<br>PSALM 45:1-17<br>PROVERBS 22:14 |
| Sep 02 Readings | ECCLESIASTES 1:1-3:22<br>2CORINTHIANS 6:1-13<br>PSALM 46:1-11<br>PROVERBS 22:15 |
| Sep 03 Readings | ECCLESIASTES 4:1-6:12<br>2CORINTHIANS 6:14-7:7<br>PSALM 47:1-9<br>PROVERBS 22:16 |
| Sep 04 Readings | ECCLESIASTES 7:1-9:18<br>2CORINTHIANS 7:8-16<br>PSALM 48:1-14<br>PROVERBS 22:17-19 |
| Sep 05 Readings | ECCLESIASTES 10:1-12:14<br>2CORINTHIANS 8:1-15<br>PSALM 49:1-20<br>PROVERBS 22:20-21 |
| Sep 06 Readings | SONG 1:1-4:16<br>2CORINTHIANS 8:16-24<br>PSALM 50:1-23<br>PROVERBS 22:22-23 |
| Sep 07 Readings | SONG 5:1-8:14<br>2CORINTHIANS 9:1-15<br>PSALM 51:1-19<br>PROVERBS 22:24-25 |
| Sep 08 Readings | ISAIAH 1:1-2:22<br>2CORINTHIANS 10:1-18<br>PSALM 52:1-9<br>PROVERBS 22:26-27 |
| Sep 09 Readings | ISAIAH 3:1-5:30<br>2CORINTHIANS 11:1-15<br>PSALM 53:1-6<br>PROVERBS 22:28-29 |
| Sep 10 Readings | ISAIAH 6:1-7:25<br>2CORINTHIANS 11:16-33<br>PSALM 54:1-7<br>PROVERBS 23:1-3 |
| Sep 11 Readings | ISAIAH 8:1-9:21<br>2CORINTHIANS 12:1-10<br>PSALM 55:1-23<br>PROVERBS 23:4-5 |
| Sep 12 Readings | ISAIAH 10:1-11:16<br>2CORINTHIANS 12:11-21<br>PSALM 56:1-13<br>PROVERBS 23:6-8 |
| Sep 13 Readings | ISAIAH 12:1-14:32<br>2CORINTHIANS 13:1-14<br>PSALM 57:1-11<br>PROVERBS 23:9-11 |
| Sep 14 Readings | ISAIAH 15:1-18:7<br>GALATIANS 1:1-24<br>PSALM 58:1-11<br>PROVERBS 23:12 |
| Sep 15 Readings | ISAIAH 19:1-21:17<br>GALATIANS 2:1-16<br>PSALM 59:1-17<br>PROVERBS 23:13-14 |
| Sep 16 Readings | ISAIAH 22:1-24:23<br>GALATIANS 2:17-3:9<br>PSALM 60:1-12<br>PROVERBS 23:15-16 |
| Sep 17 Readings | ISAIAH 25:1-28:13<br>GALATIANS 3:10-22<br>PSALM 61:1-8<br>PROVERBS 23:17-18 |
| Sep 18 Readings | ISAIAH 28:14-30:11<br>GALATIANS 3:23-4:31<br>PSALM 62:1-12<br>PROVERBS 23:19-21 |
| Sep 19 Readings | ISAIAH 30:12-33:9<br>GALATIANS 5:1-12<br>PSALM 63:1-11<br>PROVERBS 23:22 |
| Sep 20 Readings | ISAIAH 33:10-36:22<br>GALATIANS 5:13-26<br>PSALM 64:1-10<br>PROVERBS 23:23 |
| Sep 21 Readings | ISAIAH 37:1-38:22<br>GALATIANS 6:1-18<br>PSALM 65:1-13<br>PROVERBS 23:24 |
| Sep 22 Readings | ISAIAH 39:1-41:16<br>EPHESIANS 1:1-23<br>PSALM 66:1-20<br>PROVERBS 23:25-28 |

| | |
|---|---|
| Sep 23 Readings | ISAIAH 41:17-43:13<br>EPHESIANS 2:1-22<br>PSALM 67:1-7<br>PROVERBS 23:29-35 |
| Sep 24 Readings | ISAIAH 43:14-45:10<br>EPHESIANS 3:1-21<br>PSALM 68:1-18<br>PROVERBS 24:1-2 |
| Sep 25 Readings | ISAIAH 45:11-48:11<br>EPHESIANS 4:1-16<br>PSALM 68:19-35<br>PROVERBS 24:3-4 |
| Sep 26 Readings | ISAIAH 48:12-50:11<br>EPHESIANS 4:17-32<br>PSALM 69:1-18<br>PROVERBS 24:5-6 |
| Sep 27 Readings | ISAIAH 51:1-53:12<br>EPHESIANS 5:1-33<br>PSALM 69:19-36<br>PROVERBS 24:7 |
| Sep 28 Readings | ISAIAH 54:1-57:14<br>EPHESIANS 6:1-24<br>PSALM 70:1-5<br>PROVERBS 24:8 |
| Sep 29 Readings | ISAIAH 57:15-59:21<br>PHILIPPIANS 1:1-26<br>PSALM 71:1-24<br>PROVERBS 24:9-10 |
| Sep 30 Readings | ISAIAH 60:1-62:5<br>PHILIPPIANS 1:27-2:18<br>PSALM 72:1-20<br>PROVERBS 24:11-12 |
| Oct 01 Readings | ISAIAH 62:6-65:25<br>PHILIPPIANS 2:19-3:3<br>PSALM 73:1-28<br>PROVERBS 24:13-14 |
| Oct 02 Readings | ISAIAH 66:1-24<br>PHILIPPIANS 3:4-21<br>PSALM 74:1-23<br>PROVERBS 24:15-16 |
| Oct 03 Readings | JEREMIAH 1:1-2:30<br>PHILIPPIANS 4:1-23<br>PSALM 75:1-10<br>PROVERBS 24:17-20 |

| | |
|---|---|
| Oct 04 Readings | JEREMIAH 2:31-4:18<br>COLOSSIANS 1:1-17<br>PSALM 76:1-12<br>PROVERBS 24:21-22 |
| Oct 05 Readings | JEREMIAH 4:19-6:15<br>COLOSSIANS 1:18-2:7<br>PSALM 77:1-20<br>PROVERBS 24:23-25 |
| Oct 06 Readings | JEREMIAH 6:16-8:7<br>COLOSSIANS 2:8-23<br>PSALM 78:1-31<br>PROVERBS 24:26 |
| Oct 07 Readings | JEREMIAH 8:8-9:26<br>COLOSSIANS 3:1-17<br>PSALM 78:32-55<br>PROVERBS 24:27 |
| Oct 08 Readings | JEREMIAH 10:1-11:23<br>COLOSSIANS 3:18-4:18<br>PSALM 78:56-72<br>PROVERBS 24:28-29 |
| Oct 09 Readings | JEREMIAH 12:1-14:10<br>1THESSALONIANS 1:1-2:8<br>PSALM 79:1-13<br>PROVERBS 24:30-34 |
| Oct 10 Readings | JEREMIAH 14:11-16:15<br>1THESSALONIANS 2:9-3:13<br>PSALM 80:1-19<br>PROVERBS 25:1-5 |
| Oct 11 Readings | JEREMIAH 16:16-18:23<br>1THESSALONIANS 4:1-5:3<br>PSALM 81:1-16<br>PROVERBS 25:6-8 |
| Oct 12 Readings | JEREMIAH 19:1-21:14<br>1THESSALONIANS 5:4-28<br>PSALM 82:1-8<br>PROVERBS 25:9-10 |
| Oct 13 Readings | JEREMIAH 22:1-23:20<br>2THESSALONIANS 1:1-12<br>PSALM 83:1-18<br>PROVERBS 25:11-14 |
| Oct 14 Readings | JEREMIAH 23:21-25:38<br>2THESSALONIANS 2:1-17<br>PSALM 84:1-12<br>PROVERBS 25:15 |

| | |
|---|---|
| Oct 15 Readings | JEREMIAH 26:1-27:22<br>2THESSALONIANS 3:1-18<br>PSALM 85:1-13<br>PROVERBS 25:16 |
| Oct 16 Readings | JEREMIAH 28:1-29:32<br>1TIMOTHY 1:1-20<br>PSALM 86:1-17<br>PROVERBS 25:17 |
| Oct 17 Readings | JEREMIAH 30:1-31:26<br>1TIMOTHY 2:1-15<br>PSALM 87:1-7<br>PROVERBS 25:18-19 |
| Oct 18 Readings | JEREMIAH 31:27-32:44<br>1TIMOTHY 3:1-16<br>PSALM 88:1-18<br>PROVERBS 25:20-22 |
| Oct 19 Readings | JEREMIAH 33:1-34:22<br>1TIMOTHY 4:1-16<br>PSALM 89:1-13<br>PROVERBS 25:23-24 |
| Oct 20 Readings | JEREMIAH 35:1-36:32<br>1TIMOTHY 5:1-25<br>PSALM 89:14-37<br>PROVERBS 25:25-27 |
| Oct 21 Readings | JEREMIAH 37:1-38:28<br>1TIMOTHY 6:1-21<br>PSALM 89:38-52<br>PROVERBS 25:28 |
| Oct 22 Readings | JEREMIAH 39:1-41:18<br>2TIMOTHY 1:1-18<br>PSALM 90:1-91:16<br>PROVERBS 26:1-2 |
| Oct 23 Readings | JEREMIAH 42:1-44:23<br>2TIMOTHY 2:1-21<br>PSALM 92:1-93:5<br>PROVERBS 26:3-5 |
| Oct 24 Readings | JEREMIAH 44:24-47:7<br>2TIMOTHY 2:22-3:17<br>PSALM 94:1-23<br>PROVERBS 26:6-8 |
| Oct 25 Readings | JEREMIAH 48:1-49:22<br>2TIMOTHY 4:1-22<br>PSALM 95:1-96:13<br>PROVERBS 26:9-12 |
| Oct 26 Readings | JEREMIAH 49:23-50:46<br>TITUS 1:1-16<br>PSALM 97:1-98:9<br>PROVERBS 26:13-16 |
| Oct 27 Readings | JEREMIAH 51:1-53<br>TITUS 2:1-15<br>PSALM 99:1-9<br>PROVERBS 26:17 |
| Oct 28 Readings | JEREMIAH 51:54-52:34<br>TITUS 3:1-15<br>PSALM 100:1-5<br>PROVERBS 26:18-19 |
| Oct 29 Readings | LAMENTATIONS 1:1-2:22<br>PHILEMON 1:1-25<br>PSALM 101:1-8<br>PROVERBS 26:20 |
| Oct 30 Readings | LAMENTATIONS 3:1-66<br>HEBREWS 1:1-14<br>PSALM 102:1-28<br>PROVERBS 26:21-22 |
| Oct 31 Readings | LAMENTATIONS 4:1-5:22<br>HEBREWS 2:1-18<br>PSALM 103:1-22<br>PROVERBS 26:23 |
| Nov 01 Readings | EZEKIEL 1:1-3:15<br>HEBREWS 3:1-19<br>PSALM 104:1-23<br>PROVERBS 26:24-26 |
| Nov 02 Readings | EZEKIEL 3:16-6:14<br>HEBREWS 4:1-16<br>PSALM 104:24-35<br>PROVERBS 26:27 |
| Nov 03 Readings | EZEKIEL 7:1-9:11<br>HEBREWS 5:1-14<br>PSALM 105:1-15<br>PROVERBS 26:28 |
| Nov 04 Readings | EZEKIEL 10:1-11:25<br>HEBREWS 6:1-20<br>PSALM 105:16-36<br>PROVERBS 27:1-2 |
| Nov 05 Readings | EZEKIEL 12:1-14:11<br>HEBREWS 7:1-17<br>PSALM 105:37-45<br>PROVERBS 27:3 |

| Nov 06 Readings | EZEKIEL 14:12-16:41<br>HEBREWS 7:18-28<br>PSALM 106:1-12<br>PROVERBS 27:4-6 |
|---|---|
| Nov 07 Readings | EZEKIEL 16:42-17:24<br>HEBREWS 8:1-13<br>PSALM 106:13-31<br>PROVERBS 27:7-9 |
| Nov 08 Readings | EZEKIEL 18:1-19:14<br>HEBREWS 9:1-10<br>PSALM 106:32-48<br>PROVERBS 27:10 |
| Nov 09 Readings | EZEKIEL 20:1-49<br>HEBREWS 9:11-28<br>PSALM 107:1-43<br>PROVERBS 27:11 |
| Nov 10 Readings | EZEKIEL 21:1-22:31<br>HEBREWS 10:1-17<br>PSALM 108:1-13<br>PROVERBS 27:12 |
| Nov 11 Readings | EZEKIEL 23:1-49<br>HEBREWS 10:18-39<br>PSALM 109:1-31<br>PROVERBS 27:13 |
| Nov 12 Readings | EZEKIEL 24:1-26:21<br>HEBREWS 11:1-16<br>PSALM 110:1-7<br>PROVERBS 27:14 |
| Nov 13 Readings | EZEKIEL 27:1-28:26<br>HEBREWS 11:17-31<br>PSALM 111:1-10<br>PROVERBS 27:15-16 |
| Nov 14 Readings | EZEKIEL 29:1-30:26<br>HEBREWS 11:32-12:13<br>PSALM 112:1-10<br>PROVERBS 27:17 |
| Nov 15 Readings | EZEKIEL 31:1-32:32<br>HEBREWS 12:14-29<br>PSALM 113:1-114:8<br>PROVERBS 27:18-20 |
| Nov 16 Readings | EZEKIEL 33:1-34:31<br>HEBREWS 13:1-25<br>PSALM 115:1-18<br>PROVERBS 27:21-22 |
| Nov 17 Readings | EZEKIEL 35:1-36:38<br>JAMES 1:1-18<br>PSALM 116:1-19<br>PROVERBS 27:23-27 |
| Nov 18 Readings | EZEKIEL 37:1-38:23<br>JAMES 1:19-2:17<br>PSALM 117:1-2<br>PROVERBS 28:1 |
| Nov 19 Readings | EZEKIEL 39:1-40:27<br>JAMES 2:18-3:18<br>PSALM 118:1-18<br>PROVERBS 28:2 |
| Nov 20 Readings | EZEKIEL 40:28-41:26<br>JAMES 4:1-17<br>PSALM 118:19-29<br>PROVERBS 28:3-5 |
| Nov 21 Readings | EZEKIEL 42:1-43:27<br>JAMES 5:1-20<br>PSALM 119:1-16<br>PROVERBS 28:6-7 |
| Nov 22 Readings | EZEKIEL 44:1-45:12<br>1PETER 1:1-12<br>PSALM 119:17-32<br>PROVERBS 28:8-10 |
| Nov 23 Readings | EZEKIEL 45:13-46:24<br>1PETER 1:13-2:10<br>PSALM 119:33-48<br>PROVERBS 28:11 |
| Nov 24 Readings | EZEKIEL 47:1-48:35<br>1PETER 2:11-3:7<br>PSALM 119:49-64<br>PROVERBS 28:12-13 |
| Nov 25 Readings | DANIEL 1:1-2:23<br>1PETER 3:8-4:6<br>PSALM 119:65-80<br>PROVERBS 28:14 |
| Nov 26 Readings | DANIEL 2:24-3:30<br>1PETER 4:7-5:14<br>PSALM 119:81-96<br>PROVERBS 28:15-16 |
| Nov 27 Readings | DANIEL 4:1-37<br>2PETER 1:1-21<br>PSALM 119:97-112<br>PROVERBS 28:17-18 |
| Nov 28 Readings | DANIEL 5:1-31<br>2PETER 2:1-22<br>PSALM 119:113-128<br>PROVERBS 28:19-20 |

| | |
|---|---|
| Nov 29 Readings | DANIEL 6:1-28<br>2PETER 3:1-18<br>PSALM 119:129-152<br>PROVERBS 28:21-22 |
| Nov 30 Readings | DANIEL 7:1-28<br>1JOHN 1:1-10<br>PSALM 119:153-176<br>PROVERBS 28:23-24 |
| Dec 01 Readings | DANIEL 8:1-27<br>1JOHN 2:1-17<br>PSALM 120:1-7<br>PROVERBS 28:25-26 |
| Dec 02 Readings | DANIEL 9:1-11:1<br>1JOHN 2:18-3:6<br>PSALM 121:1-8<br>PROVERBS 28:27-28 |
| Dec 03 Readings | DANIEL 11:2-35<br>1JOHN 3:7-24<br>PSALM 122:1-9<br>PROVERBS 29:1 |
| Dec 04 Readings | DANIEL 11:36-12:13<br>1JOHN 4:1-21<br>PSALM 123:1-4<br>PROVERBS 29:2-4 |
| Dec 05 Readings | HOSEA 1:1-3:5<br>1JOHN 5:1-21<br>PSALM 124:1-8<br>PROVERBS 29:5-8 |
| Dec 06 Readings | HOSEA 4:1-5:15<br>2JOHN 1:1-13<br>PSALM 125:1-5<br>PROVERBS 29:9-11 |
| Dec 07 Readings | HOSEA 6:1-9:17<br>3JOHN 1:1-15<br>PSALM 126:1-6<br>PROVERBS 29:12-14 |
| Dec 08 Readings | HOSEA 10:1-14:9<br>JUDE 1:1-25<br>PSALM 127:1-5<br>PROVERBS 29:15-17 |
| Dec 09 Readings | JOEL 1:1-3:21<br>REVELATION 1:1-20<br>PSALM 128:1-6<br>PROVERBS 29:18 |
| Dec 10 Readings | AMOS 1:1-3:15<br>REVELATION 2:1-17<br>PSALM 129:1-8<br>PROVERBS 29:19-20 |
| Dec 11 Readings | AMOS 4:1-6:14<br>REVELATION 2:18-3:6<br>PSALM 130:1-8<br>PROVERBS 29:21-22 |
| Dec 12 Readings | AMOS 7:1-9:15<br>REVELATION 3:7-22<br>PSALM 131:1-3<br>PROVERBS 29:23 |
| Dec 13 Readings | OBADIAH 1:1-21<br>REVELATION 4:1-11<br>PSALM 132:1-18<br>PROVERBS 29:24-25 |
| Dec 14 Readings | JONAH 1:1-4:11<br>REVELATION 5:1-14<br>PSALM 133:1-3<br>PROVERBS 29:26-27 |
| Dec 15 Readings | MICAH 1:1-4:13<br>REVELATION 6:1-17<br>PSALM 134:1-3<br>PROVERBS 30:1-4 |
| Dec 16 Readings | MICAH 5:1-7:20<br>REVELATION 7:1-17<br>PSALM 135:1-21<br>PROVERBS 30:5-6 |
| Dec 17 Readings | NAHUM 1:1-3:19<br>REVELATION 8:1-13<br>PSALM 136:1-26<br>PROVERBS 30:7-9 |
| Dec 18 Readings | HABAKKUK 1:1-3:19<br>REVELATION 9:1-21<br>PSALM 137:1-9<br>PROVERBS 30:10 |
| Dec 19 Readings | ZEPHANIAH 1:1-3:20<br>REVELATION 10:1-11<br>PSALM 138:1-8<br>PROVERBS 30:11-14 |
| Dec 20 Readings | HAGGAI 1:1-2:23<br>REVELATION 11:1-19<br>PSALM 139:1-24<br>PROVERBS 30:15-16 |

| | |
|---|---|
| Dec 21 Readings | ZECHARIAH 1:1-21<br>REVELATION 12:1-17<br>PSALM 140:1-13<br>PROVERBS 30:17 |
| Dec 22 Readings | ZECHARIAH 2:1-3:10<br>REVELATION 13:1-18<br>PSALM 141:1-10<br>PROVERBS 30:18-20 |
| Dec 23 Readings | ZECHARIAH 4:1-5:11<br>REVELATION 14:1-20<br>PSALM 142:1-7<br>PROVERBS 30:21-23 |
| Dec 24 Readings | ZECHARIAH 6:1-7:14<br>REVELATION 15:1-8<br>PSALM 143:1-12<br>PROVERBS 30:24-28 |
| Dec 25 Readings | ZECHARIAH 8:1-23<br>REVELATION 16:1-21<br>PSALM 144:1-15<br>PROVERBS 30:29-31 |
| Dec 26 Readings | ZECHARIAH 9:1-17<br>REVELATION 17:1-18<br>PSALM 145:1-21<br>PROVERBS 30:32 |
| Dec 27 Readings | ZECHARIAH 10:1-11:17<br>REVELATION 18:1-24<br>PSALM 146:1-10<br>PROVERBS 30:33 |
| Dec 28 Readings | ZECHARIAH 12:1-13:9<br>REVELATION 19:1-21<br>PSALM 147:1-20<br>PROVERBS 31:1-7 |
| Dec 29 Readings | ZECHARIAH 14:1-21<br>REVELATION 20:1-15<br>PSALM 148:1-14<br>PROVERBS 31:8-9 |
| Dec 30 Readings | MALACHI 1:1-2:17<br>REVELATION 21:1-27<br>PSALM 149:1-9<br>PROVERBS 31:10-24 |
| Dec 31 Readings | MALACHI 3:1-4:6<br>REVELATION 22:1-21<br>PSALM 150:1-6<br>PROVERBS 31:25-31 |

# NOTE PAD

Date: _____

_____

_____

_____

_____

_____

_____

_____

_____

_____

_____

_____

_____

_____

_____

_____

_____

_____

_____

_____

# NOTE PAD

Date: _____

_____

_____

_____

_____

_____

_____

_____

_____

_____

_____

_____

_____

_____

_____

_____

_____

_____

_____

# NOTE PAD

Date: _____

_____

_____

_____

_____

_____

_____

_____

_____

_____

_____

_____

_____

_____

_____

_____

_____

_____

_____

_____

# NOTE PAD

Date: _____

_____
_____
_____
_____
_____
_____
_____
_____
_____
_____
_____
_____
_____
_____
_____
_____
_____
_____
_____

# NOTE PAD

Date: _____

_____

_____

_____

_____

_____

_____

_____

_____

_____

_____

_____

_____

_____

_____

_____

_____

_____

_____

_____

# NOTE PAD

Date: _____

# NOTE PAD

Date: _____

# NOTE PAD

Date: _____

# NOTE PAD

Date: _____

# NOTE PAD

Date: _____

# NOTE PAD

Date: _____

_____
_____
_____
_____
_____
_____
_____
_____
_____
_____
_____
_____
_____
_____
_____
_____
_____
_____
_____
_____

# NOTE PAD

Date: _____

_____
_____
_____
_____
_____
_____
_____
_____
_____
_____
_____
_____
_____
_____
_____
_____
_____
_____
_____

# What are your favorite bible verses?

### ( Write down your favorite scriptures )

**John 3:16:** For God so loved the world that he gave his one and only Son, that whoever believes in him shall not perish but have eternal life.

_____

_____

_____

_____

_____

_____

_____

_____

_____

_____

_____

_____

_____

_____

_____

_____

_____

_____

# What are your favorite bible verses?

## ( Write down your favorite scriptures )

the Sword of the Spirit,
which is the
**Word of God**
Ephesians 6:17

*Unscramble the words and write them in the corresponding blanks. Then take the letters in the circles and arrange them to find the solution to the puzzle.*

EECAP    P E (A) C E

TAFIH    F A (I) T H

SLGEEENSNT    G E N T L E N E (S) S

DESONSGO    G O O D N (E) S (S)

MEEPTNEARC    (T) E (M) P E R A N C E

EMESKNSE    M E E (K) N E (S) S

EVOL    L O V (E)

YJO    (J) O Y

GIGUNFRNFESLO    L O N G S (U) F F E R I N G

✝

*Fruit of the Spirit - How we get it.*

J E S U S   M A K E S   I T .

www.ingramcontent.com/pod-product-compliance
Lightning Source LLC
Chambersburg PA
CBHW081511040426
42447CB00013B/3184